A Photo Gallery

HIGHWAY BUSES
of the 20th Century

D0869021

William A. Luke and Linda L. Metler

Iconografix
Photo Gallery Series

Iconografix
PO Box 446
Hudson, Wisconsin 54016 USA

Library of Congress Control Number: 2004102358

ISBN 1-58388-121-2

04 05 06 07 08 09 5 4 3 2 1

Printed in China

Cover and book design by Dan Perry

Copyedited by Suzie Helberg

Cover Photos:

Upper Left: California was the scene of many early bus companies. Note the use of the hood and running board for baggage.

Upper Middle: The Greyhound Scenicruiser, introduced in 1953, was one of America's most famous buses. It featured a deck-and-a-half design and passenger appeal.

Upper Right: One of the most modern bus designs was the Model J4500 built by Motor Coach Industries. It has become popular among a number of long-distance bus companies.

Center: American bus manufacturers found it wise to change designs to compete with European manufacturers. Prevost Car Inc. presented the H series coaches in the latter part of the twentieth century. Mid-American Coaches, like many companies operating tours and charter service, featured futuristic graphics.

Book Proposals

Iconografix is a publishing company specializing in books for transportation enthusiasts. We publish in a number of different areas, including Automobiles, Auto Racing, Buses, Construction Equipment, Emergency Equipment, Farming Equipment, Railroads & Trucks. The Iconografix imprint is constantly growing and expanding into new subject areas.

Authors, editors, and knowledgeable enthusiasts in the field of transportation history are invited to contact the Editorial Department at Iconografix, Inc., PO Box 446, Hudson, WI 54016.

Bibliography

2000 *Bus Industry Chronicle*, William A. Luke
1988 *The Bus World Encyclopedia of Buses*, Ed Stauss
1987 *Modern Intercity Coaches*, Larry Plachno
1989 *The Complete Encyclopedia of Commercial Vehicles*, G. N. Georgano; G. Marshal Naul
2001 *Greyhound Canada: Its History and Coaches*, Brian W. Grams and Donald M. Bain
1965-1996 *Bus Ride* magazines
1972-1996 *Bus Industry Directory*
Motor Coach Age, various issues
Bus Transportation Magazine, various issues
Russell's Official Bus Guide, various issues
Leave the Driving to Us: A History of Greyhound Line of Canada, E. J. Hart
The Brewster Story: From Pack Train to Tour Bus, E. J. Hart
A Photographic History, Jack Rhodes
Iconografix Photo Archive Books, various editions

Table of Contents

Acknowledgments

Don Coffin, Greyhound Bus Historian, Hawley, Pennsylvania
Brian Grams, Bus Historian, Calgary, Alberta
Tom Jones, Motor Bus Society, Clark, New Jersey
Paul Leger, President, Bus History Association, Halifax, Nova Scotia
Peter Newgard, President, Canadian Transit Heritage Foundation

ABOUT THE AUTHORS

Bill Luke is a veteran of more than 50 years in the bus industry. He began his career with Jefferson Transportation Company, first as a ticket seller in Rochester, Minnesota, then soon afterward serving in various operations, traffic and management positions at the company's headquarters in Minneapolis. He was also employed with Empire Lines in Spokane, Washington, as an assistant manager.

Most of Bill's bus industry experience has been in the publication field. Bill and his wife, Adelene, owned Friendship Publications, publishing a trade journal, *Bus Ride* and several directories. The company also conducted a number of seminars.

The bus industry has been Bill's avocation since he was in grade school. He has traveled widely in the United States and Canada as well as more than 70 overseas countries.

Bill has collected considerable research material, photographs and other information about bus transportation, and this has helped make this book a possibility.

Bill has written *Bus Industry Chronicle*, an in-depth history of the entire U.S. and Canadian bus industry. He has also authored or co-authored nine Photo Archive books published by Iconografix, Inc. These books contain bus industry history through pictures, most of which are from Bill's collection.

Linda L. Metler worked for Friendship Publications for a number of years and became very familiar with the bus industry. She wrote countless articles and traveled considerably to visit bus companies interviewing owners and management people as well as taking photographs.

She enjoys writing and has a special interest in computers. These talents have been helpful in compiling and completing this book. It is her first book project, but it is very possible other books will follow.

Bill wishes to acknowledge the patience and assistance of his wife, Adelene, during the time this book was being produced. Her proofreading is also recognized.

In addition, Linda's husband, Don, has been supportive of Linda's many hours devoted to this book's completion.

Introduction

This book is a picture history of the bus industry. There has been an attempt to include pictures of as many bus manufacturers and bus models as possible, including the different models that were used extensively as well as some that were unusual. There also has been an attempt to represent as many interesting bus companies, bus routes, and other facts as possible.

In the early years there were countless bus manufacturers, some of them producing less than 10 buses a year. Often it has been impossible to find pictures of these buses or any information about them, but whatever pictures were available we have included in this book. Many of these pictures have never been published before. It has been one of the objectives to present as many pictures as possible that would be new to the readers of this book.

This is not meant to be a detailed historical account. It is produced for enjoyable reading and reminiscing about the buses that helped make the industry what it is today. The space allowed for information about the various buses, as well as the history, is limited. In the early years much of the information about the bus industry was not documented, but every effort to find information has been pursued through old publications, books, timetables, maps and advertisements as well as information from former bus industry personnel. All attempts were made to present accurate information and dates, but different historical accounts don't always agree on the facts. Those interested in a more detailed history of the entire bus industry might enjoy *Bus Industry Chronicle*, another book written by William A. Luke. This and other sources used to obtain information for this book are listed in the Bibliography.

The help of many bus historians and others and their large resource files has been appreciated. Names of these sources are also included in the Bibliography and Acknowledgments. An Index provides names of the buses, bus companies, manufacturers and other special information.

This book features the intercity, charter, tour and sightseeing bus industry.

This book complements several of the Photo Archive books on bus history that have been produced by Iconografix in recent years.

Touring Cars and Trucks

Buses designed for intercity travel did not take hold early in the history of the bus industry. What would come to be known as intercity buses were used nearly exclusively for sightseeing, primarily within cities, and by hotels and resorts for transporting guests to and from the railroad stations. It wasn't until roadways improved and tires became more reliable that buses ventured away from the cities.

Motorized buses first began to appear in the early 1900s following the invention of the internal combustion engine. Buses offered several advantages over traditional horse-drawn vehicles; they could carry a number of passengers, were able to travel faster than horse-bus services and were able to offer a number of points of interest to customers on a tour schedule.

In the early days buses operating between towns were few and far between. What routes existed were sometimes an expansion of a horse-drawn operation, a small trucking venture or a livery. Even though the motorbus was innovative, the use of intercity buses was restricted because of the condition of the roads, which were often bumpy, dusty and impassable in

California was the scene of many early bus companies. This was a large Locomobile touring car of the Imperial Valley Stage Company in 1913. Note the use of the hood and running board for baggage.

The Mack brothers of Brooklyn, New York built this sightseeing bus in 1902. This 24-horsepower, 13-passenger vehicle was regarded as the first bus in America. It saw service carrying sightseers in Brooklyn.

wet weather. In addition, little opportunity existed for intercity buses because the railroads connected to every small city.

Early buses were usually either enlarged passenger automobiles or homemade bodies on truck chassis. Most were open-top vehicles or canvas canopied, with seats consisting of benches that spanned the width of the bus.

The first buses had hard rubber tires, which restricted their speed and often yielded an uncomfortable ride. The use of pneumatic tires provided a big breakthrough in ride comfort and tire reliability, helping to make buses more acceptable for travel.

Mack Brothers built the first passenger bus. The earliest Mack buses generally had 24-horsepower, four-cylinder gasoline engines. With a speed between 12 and 20 miles per hour they carried 18 to 20 passengers and consumed a gallon of gasoline every seven miles.

In the early 1900s good roads were few. In 1912 there were only about 2 1/2 million miles of road in the United States. Improvements to the road system would be important for the advancement of the bus, opening up the opportunity for buses to operate between towns. In 1916 the Federal Aid Road Act helped improve the national road system, with the federal government paying 50 percent of the actual cost of road building up to $10,000 per mile. There was also an effort to improve roads in Canada, with the first important road opening in 1917, joining Toronto and Hamilton, Ontario.

Though roads were improving, including some lengthy concrete-surfaced highways, the bus industry still faced challenges. Cold winter weather and snow-clogged roads caused problems. A number of companies had their own snowplows and would clear the roads before highway crews could do so. Blankets were often carried on the buses to keep passengers warm. And, although buses kept improving, breakdowns on the road were still frequent. Drivers often had to double as mechanics in order to fix the bus en route and complete the trip.

The distinctive Mack Model AC bulldog chassis was an early Mack sightseeing model. This bus was in operation in New York City circa 1913. *Mack Museum*

In spite of all the challenges, the improvements to roads and the enhancement of the buses themselves encouraged many enterprising individuals to start bus lines, mostly small ones. Some companies bought trucks and mounted locally made passenger bodies, but many utilized large touring cars, often with sections added in the middle to stretch their size. As early as 1911 large touring cars were operated by Owosso-Flint Bus Company between Owosso and Flint, Michigan, a distance of 25 miles. There were many other companies operating on short-distance service between towns.

There were no real bus body manufacturers until about 1915. Before that the building of bus bodies was a hit-and-miss proposition. Bus companies managed to find someone to build a body,

The St. Alice Hotel in Harrison Hot Springs, British Columbia used this handsome bus to transfer its passengers. It is thought that this was around 1912. Many resort hotels found buses for transferring passengers an asset to their establishments.

either on a truck chassis or by extending an automobile. The bus companies themselves also built their own bus bodies.

Though pneumatic tires had replaced hard rubber tires on buses, tire failure occurred often. The touring cars had tires that lasted only 50 miles or so, and most trips saw at least one flat tire, maybe more. Two or more spare tires were carried aboard most buses, and tires were kept at intermediate stations.

Minnesota became a leading state in the development of bus transportation in the early 1900s, possibly because of the success of the bus lines on the Mesaba Iron Range. In addition, California was a leader in establishing bus lines. Companies in these states were forerunners of the companies that eventually became the nationwide Greyhound bus system.

One bus line began operating in Hibbing, Minnesota in 1914. The bus line's first vehicle was a Hupmobile touring sedan. A couple of years later the founders, Carl Eric Wickman and Andy Ander-

Early intercity buses were small touring cars. This one, a popular Model T Ford, was said to be operating in 1911 in California. Many companies used the words "stage lines" in their company names, a term that began with pioneer stagecoach operations.

Hotels found buses useful in transferring passengers between the hotel and railroad stations, as well as for sightseeing. San Diego's famous U.S. Grant Hotel had this Mack double-deck bus in service in 1910.

Rio Vista Stage was a pioneer bus company in California operating a Sacramento-Rio Vista route. An extended closed passenger car was one of its first buses in 1919. Tires were not reliable in those days; therefore, several extra ones were always carried. *Warren Miller collection*

son, incorporated the line and became the Mesaba Transportation Company. This was considered to be the beginning of Greyhound Lines.

National parks in the United States and Canada opened up a new era of sightseeing. Bus service in the parks saw a vast expansion from about 1913 to 1920. Glacier Transportation Co. in Montana's Glacier National Park was reported to have buses in service in 1913. Brewster Transport Company of Banff, Alberta placed five Overland touring cars in sightseeing service in Banff National Park in 1915. In 1917 a fleet of 116 White touring coaches was acquired to provide service in Yellowstone National Park. At the time the fleet of the Yellowstone Park Company was believed to be the largest bus fleet in the country. The Fred Harvey Company began using buses for tours in the Grand Canyon and Santa Fe, New Mexico areas prior to 1920.

Auto Interurban Company of Spokane, Washington was one of the early bus companies of the Pacific Northwest. It began running buses in 1913. One of the company's first buses was this closed-body bus with hard rubber tires. A local body builder most likely built this bus.

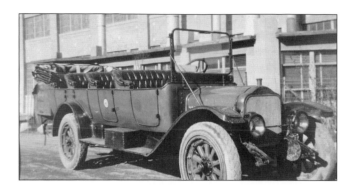

Yellowstone National Park was the first national park established in the United States. It was also one of the first national parks to operate sightseeing service. This White touring car was one of 116 similar buses acquired in 1916 for the 1917 season. Yellowstone Park Company, operator of the buses, had one of the largest fleets of buses at the time.

Mesaba Transportation Co., the company that led to the formation of the nationwide Greyhound Lines, began in Hibbing, Minnesota in 1914. The company expanded rapidly. This closed-bodied White was one of the company's buses in service in the area in 1916.

Eckland Brothers built the body of this bus on a Mack chassis for Northwestern Transportation Company of Bessemer, Michigan. Note the clerestory roof to help ventilate the bus, and the boot for baggage at the rear.

Minnesota was the scene of many early bus companies. Eckland Brothers of Minneapolis was one of the pioneer bus-body builders. The Long Prairie (Minnesota) Bus Line bought this bus, built on a White chassis, in 1918. It also carried mail, which was an added function of some of the bus companies.

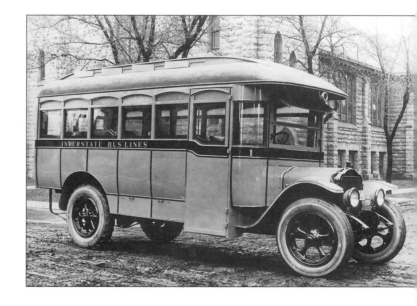

Eckland Brothers, the bus body builder of Minneapolis, Minnesota, sold buses to many areas and even Canada. This bus went to the Fort Francis-Rainey River Bus Line in Ontario, Canada in about 1918. It was built on a White chassis.

Indiana Motor Bus Co. was one of the pioneer intercity bus companies of Northern Indiana. This bus, on a locally built bus body and probably a Reo chassis, was being operated in 1919. The company began with a base in Plymouth, Indiana and later moved to South Bend, Indiana.

Left: Jefferson Highway Transportation Company, Minneapolis, Minnesota, had its start in 1919 operating routes to various Minnesota cities north of Minneapolis and St. Paul. Pictured here is one of Jefferson's first buses, a small, locally built bus body on a White chassis.

Below: Southern Wisconsin Transportation Company began in 1920 between Madison and Monroe, Wisconsin. It operated this small bus of an unknown make, presumably with a locally built body. Southern Transportation Company later extended to Freeport, Illinois. After World War II it adopted the name Badger Bus Company.

Although General Motors Corporation became an important bus builder in 1925 with its Yellow Truck & Coach Manufacturing Division, it did build some buses prior to that time. This is one of the K-31 models built for sightseeing service in 1921.

Dixie Bus Line, a small bus company in Orilla, Georgia, operated this 1925 Model K-16 bus. It was built by General Motors Corporation and could accommodate 16 passengers who entered the bus though doors on the right side.

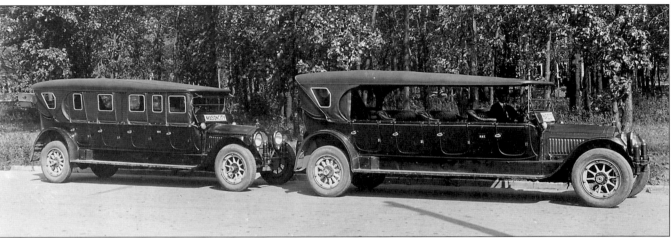

Helen Schultz Davis started Red Ball Transportation Company, Mason City, Iowa, in 1922. Two of Red Ball's original buses were these Packard touring cars used on the company's routes in Northern Iowa. Packard was an early automobile builder and various companies often used Packard touring cars as buses.

The Pierce-Arrow Motor Car Corporation in Buffalo, New York was an early bus builder, building both complete buses and chassis for buses. The North Bend Stage Line of Seattle, Washington operated these four Pierce-Arrow buses, pictured here in 1921. *E. E. "Skip" Arneson*

These three extra-large sedans were (left to right): a Cadillac of Lone Star Stages, a Studebaker of Roberson Stage Company, and a Hudson of the Fort Worth-Waco Stage Line. This picture was taken in the late 1920s. These bus companies were later sold to other companies in Texas. *Motor Bus Society*

Crown Coach Company began in 1923 as Brown Brothers Bus Line operating south out of Kansas City, Missouri. One of the early Crown buses was this large sedan-type bus, reported to be a 1928 Lincoln. Crown later was established in Joplin, Missouri and then operated a main route between Kansas City and Texarkana.

Purpose-built Buses

All through the history of the industry, bus designs were motivated by the desire to enhance performance, safety and comfort. Another important objective was to design larger buses with greater seating capacities.

Brothers Frank R. and William B. Fageol, who began Fageol Motor Co. in Oakland, California, built the first purpose-built bus, the Fageol Safety Coach, in 1922. The Safety Coach was a breakthrough for the intercity bus industry. It did not require a truck chassis, as in the past, and the body was mounted low on the chassis, resulting in a low center of gravity. The first Safety Coaches accommodated 22 passengers who entered the bus from several doors along the side. Over the years improvements were made to the Safety Coach, including an increased size, a passenger door at the front, and seats on either side of an aisle. Because of the width of the bus, the seating was arranged with one passenger seat on one side and two on the other. As greater widths were allowed in buses, two seats on one side of the aisle and two on the other became more common. Later, many bus companies saw the

Auto Interurban Company of Spokane, Washington outfitted this 1925 Fageol Safety Coach with an upper deck for passengers wishing to enjoy sightseeing or the thrill of an upper deck ride. Auto Interurban Company operated a large fleet of Fageol buses. *Werner Rosenquist collection*

In order to maintain schedules in winter months bus companies plowed snow before highway crews could do so. This Fageol Safety Coach, equipped with a snowplow, is seen on a Duluth-Twin Cities route in Minnesota in the early 1920s.

After snow was cleared on the roads, especially in the north and in Canada, buses often had a one-way passage. This White of White Bus Company, Superior, Wisconsin, is seen on the narrow road on the Scott Highway near Fort William (now Thunder Bay), Ontario. This was a typical scene in the early 1920s. Note the high-mounted headlights on the bus.

White Bus Company of Superior, Wisconsin was a pioneer bus company that operated this Fageol Safety Coach on its intercity route between Duluth and the Canadian cities of Fort William and Port Arthur, Ontario. Today the two cities are known as Thunder Bay.

advantage of the new bus and it appeared everywhere, even overseas.

In the 1920s there were hundreds of bus manufacturers in every part of the country. Some built just four or five buses a year, making it convenient for operators to buy buses locally. As the decade progressed there were more specific bus builders and that, along with the Depression, pushed many of the smaller manufacturers out of the picture.

Many engine manufacturers were around, including White Motor Co. and Mack Trucks Inc., which manufactured both engines and chassis, and Waukesha Motor Co., Buda Engine Co., Hercules Motor Corp. and Hall-Scott Engine Co., among many others. Even during this period there were many buses still being built on truck chassis. Prominent makes included Studebaker Corporation, Dodge Brothers, Ford Motor Co., White, Mack and a number of others. Hayes Manufacturing Co. (Hayes-Anderson) of Vancouver, British Columbia, also built buses.

The Yellow Coach Manufacturing Co. began in 1923. Fifth Avenue Coach Company's John Hertz and John Ritchie in New York City formed Yellow Coach. The company later became known as Yellow Truck & Coach Manufacturing Co. and also became a part of the General Motors Corporation. At first Yellow Coach built its own chassis and used bodies built by a number of different body builders. But over the years Yellow Coach also built many of its own bodies, just as Fageol Motors did.

Early buses had many features similar to those on trains, including the vented clerestory roof, rear-end grillwork like the observation car on a passenger train, and lantern lights on the back, like the rear of a train. Manufacturers were trying to make their buses look similar to trains in an effort to encourage passengers to think buses were as good as trains.

Baggage space was always a consideration. The first touring car operators often strapped baggage to the running boards and the back end. Later a container was placed on the back of the bus to accommodate baggage. Eventually the baggage was brought inside and stored on racks over the seats. These big baggage racks made the inside of the bus look dark and confined. The effect wasn't helped by the seats, which were often made of wicker with cushions on them, although this was contemporary

In the Pacific Northwest winter snows in some of the mountain passes were a challenge to buses on routes. This bus was equipped with a heavy-duty rotary plow mounted on the bus. This was pictured circa 1920.

with the furniture of the day. Throughout the 1920s and 1930s buses also had considerable space on the roof for baggage. There were ladders on the back or the side of the bus, allowing the drivers or baggage loaders to climb up on the roof. Sometimes there was a high-platform wagon to carry the baggage to the bus where it was then transferred to the roof.

In the late 1920s night coaches were used. Pickwick Stages began running its Nite Coaches on long-distance routes in 1928. The Pickwick Corporation built these buses, which had seats that could be converted into beds for night travel. There was a porter on board, similar to that on a train. However, the seating capacity was limited because the bed arrangement took up so much room when converted, keeping the Nite Coaches from being cost effective. By 1935 they had lost their appeal.

About the same time, several manufacturers developed combination buses. These buses had room in the rear for freight and seats for passengers in the front. This was done primarily because some of the branch lines of the railroads discontinued and buses were able to carry packages as well as passengers.

Eckland Brothers Company of Minneapolis, Minnesota began building buses in 1915, but later teamed with C. H. Will Motors Corp., a chassis

Fageol Motors Company of Oakland, California introduced the Safety Coach in 1922. It was totally built for bus operations and became a choice for many bus fleets. Mesaba Transportation Company of Hibbing, Minnesota operated these two Safety Coaches in the early 1920s. The first type of Safety Coach is pictured in the rear and the succeeding model in the front.

California Parlor Car Tours was one of the first companies offering bus tours. This 1924 Fageol Safety Coach is shown on the occasion of its first trip. Note the fancy canopy and grille work at the rear. This was typical of buses of that era. They were supposed to resemble railway observation cars. *Warren Miller collection*

builder. The team built many Eckland/Will buses, especially for Greyhound, in the latter part of the 1920s. They and other bus manufacturers, including Yellow Coach and White, found that mounting the engine over the front axle allowed them to increase seating capacity. Everyone acknowledged that idea and turned to that system of increasing the sizes of buses at that time.

Motor Transit Corporation, a company formed in 1926, adopted the Greyhound Lines name in 1929. This was the first big bus line consolidation program. Separate companies were brought into the Greyhound organization as divisions, making the transcontinental Greyhound system a reality.

Eugene Prevost began building buses in Ste. Claire, Quebec in 1924. There was no other specific builder in Canada at that time, although there were many companies in Canada that built a few buses. In most cases Canada relied on the United States for buses. The Canadian bus building industry was not well established until the 1930s.

The Flxible Company of Loudonville, Ohio also began building buses in 1924. The Flxible Company was not connected with any chassis or engine manufacturer, although the company had ties with some of the leaders of General Motors. Charles Kettering, who helped develop General Motors' diesel engine, was a part of the Flxible Company for many years. Unlike many of the bus builders of the day, the Flxible Company did not build automobiles or trucks, though they did build hearses and ambulances. There were also a few other companies, Fitzjohn Body Co. and The C. D. Beck & Co. particularly, that had early starts in the 1930s and were not connected with automobile or truck manufacturing. Truck and automakers White, Mack, Studebaker, Reo Motor Car Co., Pierce-Arrow Motor Car Co. and Graham Bros. also began making buses around the same time.

By the 1930s Yellow Coach was considered a very important intercity bus manufacturer, along with a number of other companies such as American Car & Foundry (ACF), White and Mack.

The Wolverton Auto Bus Company operated this White bus between Port Angeles and The Forks on Washington's Olympic Peninsula around 1925. The bus had a door at each row of seats and accommodated 12 passengers.

There was no identification on this large touring car, most likely a Hudson, which no doubt was in bus service. On the shirt of the man assumed to be the driver is the name Fort Worth Waco Stage Line. That company later became Central Texas Bus Lines. The picture was taken circa 1927.

Clyde, Ohio was the home of a little-known builder of a bus called the Clydesdale. It is pictured in 1923 at the Plum Brook Country Club in Sandusky, Ohio. The bus was a sedan type with doors along the side of the bus and seating the width of the bus. *Dale Hohler*

In the late 1920s West Texas had a number of bus companies. One was Texas Motor Lines in Fort Worth, which, at that time, had a fleet of small buses on White chassis. By 1931 Red Star Coaches acquired the company, and in 1939 it and a number of other companies merged to form Texas, New Mexico & Oklahoma (T.N.M. & O.) Coaches of Lubbock, Texas.

Cannon Ball Transportation Company of Durango, Colorado acquired these two Studebaker buses in 1926. The Studebaker Corporation, South Bend, Indiana, was an early automobile manufacturer, which began offering chassis to bus builders in 1925. Superior Body Company, Lima, Ohio, built most of the bodies for Studebaker. It was assumed that these buses had Superior bodies.

This 1926 Yellow Coach Model Y was known as an Observation Coach because the rear section had side-mounted seats facing each other and a large window for viewing. In the middle of the bus was a space for a lavatory and a galley. Yellow Manufacturing Company built the chassis but Thompson Body Company built the body. Many Model Y buses were seen throughout the country. Model X and Model Z intercity buses followed the Model Y.

Mesaba Transportation Company, Hibbing, Minnesota, was founded in 1914. It is considered the company that started the nationwide Greyhound Lines. Several of the founders left Mesaba to build the Greyhound empire. Mesaba Transportation remained a local bus service in Hibbing. In 1926, when this Thompson-bodied Yellow Coach Model Y was purchased, the company operated intercity service to Duluth, Grand Rapids, and Bemidji from Hibbing.

The Model Y bus was built by Yellow Truck & Coach Manufacturing Co. beginning in 1924. It was a model built by Yellow Coach for intercity service and proved to be very popular in the 1920s. Original Model Y buses had bodies built by a variety of bus body builders, including Thompson Body Company, which built bodies for many Yellow Coach buses. This is a 1929 Yellow Coach sold to the Central Transportation Company of Waterloo, Iowa and operated on a route between Dubuque and Fort Dodge, Iowa via Waterloo. The company later was named Black and White Transportation Co. followed by the name Iowa Coaches.

In the mid-1920s, Eckland Body Company, Minneapolis, Minnesota, continued to build buses on chassis; however, the chassis then available to bus builders were built lower. Pictured is one of the buses for the Copper Range Motor Bus Company of Houghton, Michigan circa 1927. White Motors built the chassis and the Eckland body was able to allow a lower step and more attractive body styling. Copper Range Motor Bus Company was a pioneer bus company operating in the copper mining area of the Keweenaw Peninsula of Upper Michigan.

Most buses built by the Eckland/Will team had bodies with seating for 33 passengers. This 1929 Model NL had seats for 17 passengers and an interior baggage compartment in the rear. It was one of a kind and sold to Northland Transportation Company, Minneapolis, Minnesota, which later became a Greyhound division.

Around 1927 the Minneapolis, Minnesota bus body builder Eckland Brothers teamed with C. H. Will Motors Company, a chassis manufacturer. The two companies brought about a new bus design by mounting the engine over the front axle, increasing the seating capacity of the bus. Joliet Plainfield & Aurora Transportation Company of Illinois acquired one of the new Eckland/Will buses.

Royal Rapid Lines, Madison, Wisconsin, was a company begun by the Fitzgerald Brothers, bus pioneers in Northern Minnesota. Royal Rapid Lines operated from Chicago to various cities in Northern Illinois and Wisconsin. In 1927 Royal Rapid purchased Eckland/Will buses like the one pictured here. The Fitzgerald Brothers sold Royal Rapid to Greyhound and went on to form the National City Lines empire.

Wilcox Trux Co. of Minneapolis, Minnesota built some bus chassis in the early 1920s. Most had Eckland bodies. Pictured here is a 1926 Eckland/Wilcox bus built for Northland Transportation Company, which later became Northland Greyhound Lines.

The Twin Coach Company introduced the revolutionary Model 40 bus in 1927. Most Model 40s were acquired for city service. However, intercity companies purchased some. Pictured is an intercity Model 40 demonstrator. A unique feature of the bus was its two engines, hence the name Twin Coach. *Donald Coffin collection*

This 1928 ACF Model 508-2-13-3 was a deck-and-a-half design. It was operated by the Boston & Maine Transportation Company between Boston, Massachusetts and Portland, Maine. The Boston & Maine Transportation Company was a subsidiary of the Boston & Maine Railroad.

In the late 1920s a small, short-lived bus company known as the Interstate Express operated this Studebaker bus serving Providence, Rhode Island and Boston, Massachusetts. The Studebaker Corporation built many medium-sized bus chassis for body builders. Many Studebaker buses had straight eight engines.

The Shultz Management Company of Southern New Jersey originally operated this 1927 Model AL Mack. It later became a part of the large Public Service organization, which had many bus and trolley routes throughout New Jersey.

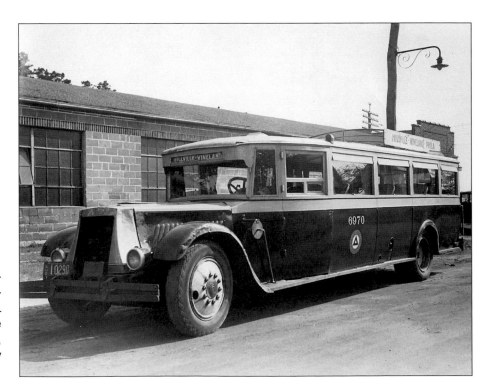

Jefferson Highway Transportation Company, Minneapolis, Minnesota, bought this Model 54 White with a Bender Body Company body in November 1928. This was a very popular intercity bus at that time and 1,300 were built by 1930. Jefferson was operating a main route between Minneapolis and Kansas City, Missouri in 1928.

Brewster Transport Company of Banff, Alberta operated this open-top sightseeing bus of the early 1920s. Brewster was established in 1892. In this picture the Banff Springs Hotel, an important landmark, is shown in the background.

Glacier Park Transportation Company in Montana acquired two 1927 Model 54 White buses with Bender bodies. The 33-passenger buses had open sides and a canvas roof that could be retracted. When entirely open, the passengers had excellent sightseeing advantages. The bus is pictured at the top of Logan Pass on the Going-to-the-Sun Highway in Glacier Park.

Three special LaSalle touring cars joined the Glacier Park (Montana) Transport Co. fleet in 1930. They were added to the eight 1927 Cadillac touring cars already in service. The LaSalle cars were used for special guests and supplemented the large fleet of White buses that were serving Glacier National Park at that time. The first motorized bus transportation began in the park in 1914.

In 1931 Mount Rainier Park Company began operating Model 54 White touring cars in sightseeing service in Mount Rainier National Park in Washington. The buses had rollback canvas tops and accommodated 13 passengers. Majestic Mount Rainier is in the background.

In 1936, 18 Model 706 White open-top sightseeing buses went into service in Glacier National Park in Montana. In the next three years, 17 more were purchased for sightseeing in Glacier. Pictured here are three of the Whites at Glacier Park Hotel. The buses were affectionately called Red Buses or Jammers. The word jammers came as a result of frequent gear changing by the drivers on the mountain roads. Most of the original Model 706 White buses were refurbished in 2001 and 2002 after more than 65 years of service.

The "Cherokee," built in 1928, was one of the most unusual buses ever built. Pickwick Stages of California operated it. In the middle was a raised observation deck, and at the rear there were seats that faced rearward for the passenger's viewing. The driver was in a "Pilot House" also at a raised level. *Motor Bus Society*

Similar to the "Cherokee" Pickwick Stages observation bus was this model with the upper deck observation. The driver was not in a raised "Pilot House" like the "Cherokee" design, but was at the normal driving position. *Motor Bus Society*

Pickwick Motor Coach Works in Los Angeles built the Nite Coach. The first Nite Coaches were operated by Pickwick Stages, a pioneer California bus company and later a long-distance bus operator throughout the West. The Nite Coach pictured here was first introduced in 1928. It had 13 compartments, each of which accommodated two people, with a dressing room and running water. Pickwick built 63 sleeper buses between 1928 and 1933. All sleeper bus service was discontinued prior to the start of World War II. *Motor Bus Society*

Columbia Pacific Lines, Inc. was one of several companies operating Nite Coach service. The short-lived company bought this bus and several others in 1933, actually the last Nite Coaches built, and operated them for two years. Pickwick Motor Coach Works in California built these large Nite Coaches.

This was one of several different bus models produced by Pickwick Motor Coach Corporation, Los Angeles, California. The first double-deck Nite Coach was built in 1928. Pickwick built a day coach called the Duplex in 1930. When used for intercity service these buses had a normal seating capacity for 58 passengers on two decks. The Duplex bus was operated on several routes, but like the Nite Coaches, they were not built in great numbers and disappeared from service after only a few years.

Trying Times and Small Buses

T he trying days of the Depression brought many challenges to the bus industry, just as they did to all businesses. Many bus company owners were their own bus drivers and mechanics, and did everything else required because there was no opportunity to build a big bus operating company. It was simply a matter of survival.

In spite of the challenges, the Depression era saw some advantages for the bus companies. Many railroads were also finding it difficult to survive and were discontinuing service, especially to smaller cities. Using smaller buses, the bus companies were able to fulfill the role of the railroad just as well and just as comfortably, and with lower fares. Buses could also go off the main line railroad route and serve other towns that never had train service. Consequently, bus companies gained some new routes and services or expanded the services they already had. There were also quite a few electric railway systems, especially in the Midwest and the east, that were having hard times, too. A number of these

Bus Number BT-1 was not exactly a bus but was a combination truck/bus. The White Motor Company built it for the Santa Fe Transportation Company of Wichita, Kansas, a subsidiary of the Atchison, Topeka and Santa Fe Railroad, in the early 1930s. At that time, many railroad companies were substituting trucks and buses on small branch railroad lines. *American Truck Historical Society*

electric railway companies began to establish their own bus lines and operate buses in the 1930s. At the same time a number of the larger railroad companies were also beginning to operate buses.

Early bus companies usually took their names from their owners' name or the area they served. The word "stage" was often incorporated into company names, signifying that buses were taking the place of earlier stagecoaches. Other terms often used in company names included coach, bus company, transit company and transportation service. Also used for bus company names were names of animals, birds, mountains and rivers in areas served.

In the 1930s more emphasis was being placed on the design of the bus, both inside and out, and the comfort of the passenger. Seats were more colorful and inviting, with reclining seats becoming the standard. The Carrier Corporation introduced air conditioning on buses in the mid-1930s, and by the end of the decade air conditioning was used universally in most large long-distance buses and also in some smaller buses.

There was also quite a bit of emphasis on paint designs for the exterior of the buses, with company names prominently shown on the sides. In the beginning Greyhound chose blue and white as its colors and featured a streamlining teardrop over the front and rear wheels. The smaller independent companies that connected with Greyhound wanted to show their allegiance to the Greyhound system. Even though they might have had only two or three buses, the smaller independent operators also painted their buses blue and white and carried the same Greyhound-looking design on the sides.

In 1936, an association of large independent bus companies was formed. It was known as The National Trailways Bus System. Trailways' paint scheme was predominantly crimson and cream. Companies closely aligned with the Trailways companies, but not members, often painted their buses using the same crimson and cream.

During this time, advertising for bus services increased. Greyhound did considerable advertising to attract business, and used the attractive appearance of its buses not only as a selling point, but also to help show that buses were no longer in the Dark Ages. The Century of Progress World's Fair in Chicago was promoted and proved to be a boost to bus travel as the Depression years faded.

Many companies went back to using elongated sedans as buses, which accommodated 10 or 11 passengers. They were mainly Buick, Chevrolet and Ford sedans, and were lengthened by various bus manufacturers. A number of new bus manufacturers entered the intercity market in the 1930s and prior to World War II. Among them were Gar Wood Industries (later acquired by General American Aerocoach Corp.), Brown Industries, Kalamazoo

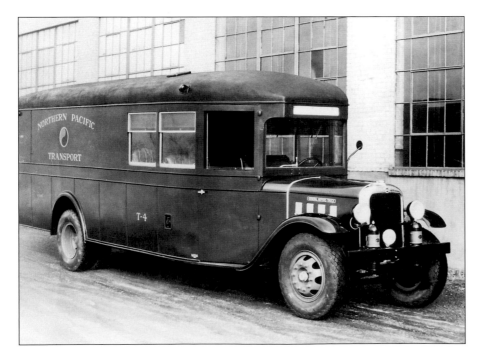

In the mid-1930s a number of railroad companies abandoned branch lines and ran replacement service with combination vehicles. This General Motors truck had seats for seven passengers and a large freight-carrying section at the rear. Eckland Body Company built the body of this vehicle for the Northern Pacific Transport Company.

In 1932, this Model BK Mack bus, equipped with a Cummins Model H diesel engine, was said to be the first bus in the United States with a diesel engine. The bus made a test trip from coast to coast. Clessie Cummins, founder of the Cummins Engine Company, Columbus, Indiana, made the trip in the bus. *C. Lyle Cummins*

Coaches, Inc., Fargo Motor Corp. and Dittmar Manufacturing Co. (DMX). Some bus manufacturers concentrated on school buses but also entered the intercity market. Superior Coach Corporation, The Wayne Works, Crown Body & Coach Corp. and Gillig Brothers were some of the manufacturers of intercity buses.

In Canada, Fort Garry Motor Body and Paint Works and Western Auto Body and Truck Works (Western Flyer) came into the bus-manufacturing picture in the mid-1930s. The buses of these two companies became very popular among many bus operators, especially in western Canada. The Fort Garry Motor Body and Paint Works later became known as Motor Coach Industries. Prevost continued bus building, marketing its buses mainly in eastern Canada.

The roads in Canada were not as modern as they were in the United States; they were rugged, still mostly gravel and often muddy. The Canadian bus manufacturers built buses rugged enough to handle the extreme road conditions as well as the Canadian winters.

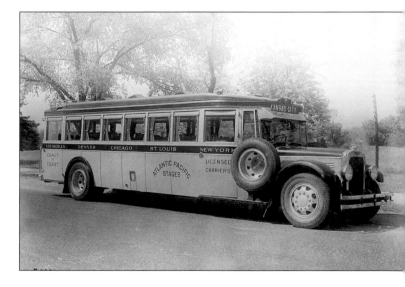

Mack Trucks built the BK chassis between 1929 and 1934. A total of 92 were built for buses. Atlantic-Pacific Stages had this Mack BK in its fleet. Colonial Stages, Cincinnati, Ohio, later purchased Atlantic-Pacific Stages, St. Louis, Missouri.

Victoria Coach Lines, Boston, Massachusetts, was a pioneer bus company in New England, which began in 1924 with a route between Boston and New York. In 1931 it operated this Yellow Coach Model Z-BI-610. New England Transportation Company purchased Victoria Coach Lines in 1932, but the Victoria name continued. The Victoria service ended in 1937 when New England Greyhound Lines bought New England Transportation Company.

Yellow Truck & Coach Manufacturing Company was one of the largest builders of buses in the United States. This Model VR 819 Yellow Coach was delivered to Tennessee Coach Company in Knoxville in 1934. This model and similar others were referred to as "Streamliners."

In 1932, Jefferson Transportation Company of Minneapolis, Minnesota considered replacing its fleet of Model 54 White buses purchased over the past few years. Rather than buy new buses, the company decided that these buses should be refurbished. The refurbishing was done in the Minneapolis shops one at a time. The result was a more streamlined bus, which helped carry the company successfully through the difficult Depression years.

Frank Martz Coach Co., Wilkes-Barre, Pennsylvania, had this 21-passenger White Model 65A bus with a streamlined Bender body in service in 1934. Martz had a sizable bus system stretching between New York and Chicago, but the company later sold the longer lines and concentrated on service in Eastern Pennsylvania and New York. Martz was one of the founders of the National Trailways Bus System. *American Truck Historical Society*

Canada Coach Lines, Hamilton, Ontario, operated this 1932 Model 613 White bus. Originally it had a low roof design, but it was heightened in the Canada Coach Lines shops. The Model 613 had an L-head, six-cylinder, 299-cubic-inch engine. Canada Coach Lines was a subsidiary of the Hamilton Street Railway Company. It began in 1923 and served many communities on the Niagara Peninsula, along with a route to Buffalo, New York. Canada Coach Lines was sold to Trentway-Wagar, Inc. in 1993.

White Star Motor Coach Company was a small bus line operating in the Peoria, Illinois area in the mid-1930s. White Star acquired this 21-passenger White with a Bender body in 1936.

Most bus manufacturers offered a line of small buses during the 1930s. Yellow Coach was one, and introduced this Model 715, which was mainly for city services. This particular Model 715 was used in the intercity service of the Hazard Jenkins Line in Kentucky in 1935.

This Model 724 Yellow Coach bus was a rarity because only four were built, all in 1935. They were originally delivered to Tri-State Coaches, Shreveport, Louisiana. A short time later they became a part of the Detroit-based Eastern Michigan Motorbuses fleet. The buses had 400-cubic-inch General Motors gasoline engines mounted in-line in the rear.

The Yellow Coach Model 742, introduced in 1937, was an intercity bus, which didn't prove popular. Only 161 were built. This Model 742, owned by Hudson Transit Corporation, Newburg, New York, was one of the first of this type built. Hudson Transit was part of the Short Line group of companies in the East and had routes from New York to Binghamton and Albany, New York.

Southeastern Greyhound Lines, Lexington, Kentucky, was one of the most important users of ACF buses, beginning in the late 1920s. This ACF Model H-9-P was added, along with four others, to the Southeastern fleet in 1936. The H-9-P had a Hall-Scott 180-horsepower under-floor engine and seated 36 passengers. Although Southeastern carried the Greyhound name, it did not become a fully owned Greyhound company until 1950.

Blue Way Lines, Springfield, Massachusetts, was a pioneer bus company operating in New England beginning in 1922. Blue Way provided service between Portland, Maine through Boston and New York City. In 1932 it became a part of the Short Line system, and in 1941 joined the National Trailways Bus System. In 1935 and 1936 Blue Way Lines acquired eight ACF Model H-9-P buses, one of which is pictured here.

The ACF Model 37-P was the flagship bus of the National Trailways Bus System companies prior to World War II. In 1938 Rio Grand Trailways of Denver, Colorado acquired five of these buses. They were powered with Hall-Scott under-floor engines.

Canadian bus companies looked to England for some of their buses in the 1930s. Colonial Coach Lines, Ottawa, Ontario, purchased this 29-passenger AEC Ranger bus in 1933. This luxury bus had a body by Metro-Cammell-Weyman Company, which, like AEC, was a British bus manufacturer.

Gray Coach Lines, a subsidiary of the Toronto Transportation Commission, was incorporated in 1927. It was formed to operate intercity services in the Toronto, Ontario area. Quite a variety of buses were in the Gray Coach fleet, including several built in England. In 1932 two buses, one of which is pictured here, entered the Gray Coach fleet. They were built on AEC Ranger chassis and Canadian Car bodies. Two more AEC Rangers were purchased the next year, but with Duple bodies also from England. The company was sold to Greyhound Canada in 1994.

A number of city transit systems operated sightseeing services in the early days of bus transportation and some were members of the Gray Line Sightseeing Association. The Ottawa (Ontario) Electric Company operated this 1938 Yellow Coach Model W.

Provincial Transport Company of Montreal, Quebec was operating this Reo 17-passenger bus on local routes in Quebec in 1938. It is believed the body was built by the Ottawa (Ontario) Car Body Company.

The Fort Garry Motor Body and Paint Works of Winnipeg, Manitoba stretched out a Packard sedan to produce this bus. It was built in 1933 and was the first bus built by the company. Eight years later the Fort Garry Motor Body and Paint Works became Motor Coach Industries.

Vancouver Island Coach Lines, Ltd. of Victoria, British Columbia bought this bus, which was built by Hayes Manufacturing Company, in 1936. It had a Model 29 PCD 35-passenger body and a British Leyland engine. Hayes was a distributor for Leyland in the 1930s. Vancouver Island Coach Line began in 1928.

Washington Motor Coach System referred to its route across Washington State and to Butte, Montana as the Northern Short Route. This bus, with what probably was a Brown Industries body, was built on an Indiana Motors Company truck chassis circa 1934. Indiana Motors, Marion, Indiana, had its beginnings in 1911 with a predecessor company. In 1933 the company moved to Cleveland, Ohio and was controlled by White Motor Company.

Union Transportation Company of Tulsa, Oklahoma added four of these Fitzjohn Duraliner buses to its fleet in March 1938. The Duraliners introduced at that time featured International or Hercules engines.

Thousand Islands Bus Line of Alexandria Bay, New York operated this 1937 Reo with a Beck Airstream body on a route leased by Central Greyhound Lines. The C. D. Beck & Co. began marketing the Airstream model in 1934. Several truck chassis were used for Airstream bodies. *Motor Bus Society*

The C. D. Beck & Co., Sidney, Ohio, presented this new Metro Inter-City Parlor Coach using a Chevrolet chassis in 1937. It was advertised to have a Safety Steel Deck and steel exterior. It weighed less than five tons and cost $4,795.

The C. D. Beck & Co. started in 1934 with bus bodies on truck chassis. In 1936 the Cosmopolitan model was introduced. It had a front engine of several makes and a full front body. Kerrville Bus Company of Kerrville, Texas owned the Beck Cosmopolitan pictured here. Kerrville became a distributor of Beck buses and had a large Beck fleet for many years.

Consolidated Bus Lines of Bluefield, West Virginia operated this Flxible Airway bus in 1936. The Flxible Company introduced the Airway models on Chevrolet chassis in 1936. This introduction lead to The Flxible Company's leadership in small bus production for almost 20 years.

Greyhound Lines began buying Yellow Coach buses instead of Eckland/Will buses in 1939. As a result, Eckland brothers was left without its major customer. Eckland continued to build bus bodies and even built this stretched-out bus from a 1936 Buick sedan. It was built for Interstate Transportation Company of Bismarck, North Dakota.

In 1934 the Fitzjohn Body Company of Muskegon, Michigan recognized that the Depression years were creating a demand for smaller, more economical buses. The company began building stretched-out buses from sedans. More than 700 were built. Pictured here is one of the Fitzjohn Model 100 buses using a 1937 Chevrolet sedan. Route 80 Short Way Line in Pennsylvania operated this sedan bus.

Berkshire Coach Lines and Victoria Coach Lines, both of Boston, Massachusetts, operated service between Boston and New York City. The two companies were sold to New England Transportation Co. in 1929, but continued to operate independently. Ten years later the companies were sold to New England Greyhound. Berkshire had four Buick Fitzjohn Model 100 stretched-out sedan buses, one of which is pictured here. They were acquired in 1936.

Capitol Bus Company of Harrisburg, Pennsylvania purchased this Fitzjohn 1937 Chevrolet stretched-out bus. It was one of Capitol's first buses. This bus has been preserved and is now in the Museum of Bus Transportation. Capitol began in 1936 with a route between Pottsville, Pennsylvania and Harrisburg.

By the mid-1930s the Studebaker Corporation was beginning to phase out a fairly active bus-chassis building program. By 1936 some chassis were offered to bus body builders. Mullan Transportation Company in Northern Idaho operated this bus on a Model 2MB86 chassis.

The Fargo Motor Corporation, a division of the Chrysler Corporation, built a limited number of buses carrying the Fargo name between 1930 and 1933. All but two of the Fargo buses were sold to city bus companies. This Model 91 was one of the intercity Fargo buses. It was owned by Eastern Michigan Motorbuses, Detroit, and used on its Great Lakes Motor Bus Company route.

Gar Wood Industries, Detroit, Michigan, began building buses in 1936. This 20-passenger, all-aluminum intercity bus was its first bus. It had a uniquely designed front; the Ford V-8 engine was mounted in the rear. Eastern Michigan Motorbuses in Detroit ordered five of these Model CTF Gar Wood buses in 1937.

Black Hawk Transit Company, Peoria, Illinois, began serving central Illinois in 1928. Black Hawk expanded in the mid-1930s to Davenport, Iowa and Springfield and Freeport, Illinois. Black Hawk Transit Company owned this 24-passenger Brown Industries bus, which was powered by a Hercules gasoline engine.

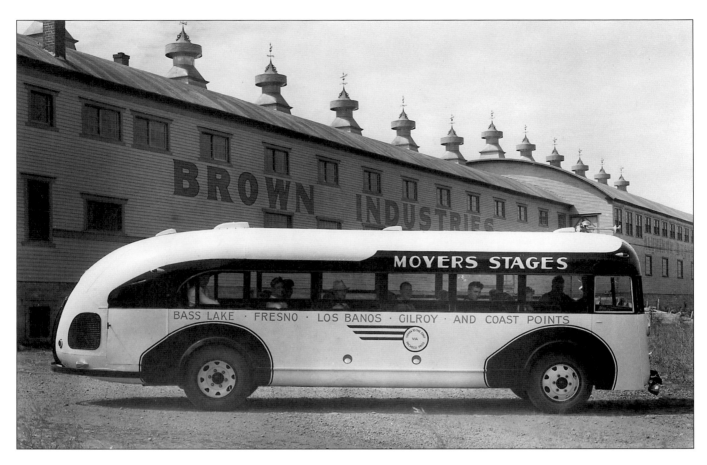

Brown Industries of Spokane, Washington built complete buses for only three years, from 1936 to 1938. Their bus was of modern design featuring frameless airplane-type construction. Ford engines, and later Hercules engines mounted in the rear, were used. Moyers Stages of Fresno, California acquired this 24-passenger model in 1936.

The DMX bus was built by the Dittmar Manufacturing Company of Chicago, Illinois between 1936 and 1940. Both intercity and transit models were built. South Plains Coaches of Post, Texas purchased this 29-passenger Hercules-powered DMX bus in 1937. South Plains Coaches was involved in a merger two years later at which time Texas, New Mexico & Oklahoma (T.N.M. & O.) Coaches of Lubbock, Texas was incorporated.

Reo Motor Car Co., Lansing, Michigan, began building trucks in 1908 and entered the bus market in the mid-1920s. Reo continued building buses for many years, mainly school and city buses. In the late 1930s the Model 309 Reo bus was announced and offered in both transit and intercity versions. It was called the Flying Cloud. Pictured here is one of four Model 309-Ps for Seashore Transportation Company of New Bern, North Carolina. *Motor Bus Society*

M. C. Foster Bus Line, Troy, Missouri, operated what was called the Mark Twain Route between St. Louis, Missouri and Southeastern Iowa. M. C. Foster began the line in 1925 with a 16-passenger bus between St. Louis and Troy. The line was extended north in the 1930s and sold to Burlington Trailways in 1943. Between 1938 and 1941, M.C. Foster Bus Line acquired six Reo Flying Cloud Model 309-P buses. Reo Motor Car Company of Lansing, Michigan, was formed in 1904 and began its truck building subsidiary in 1913. Buses were built soon afterward, but bus production ended in 1955.

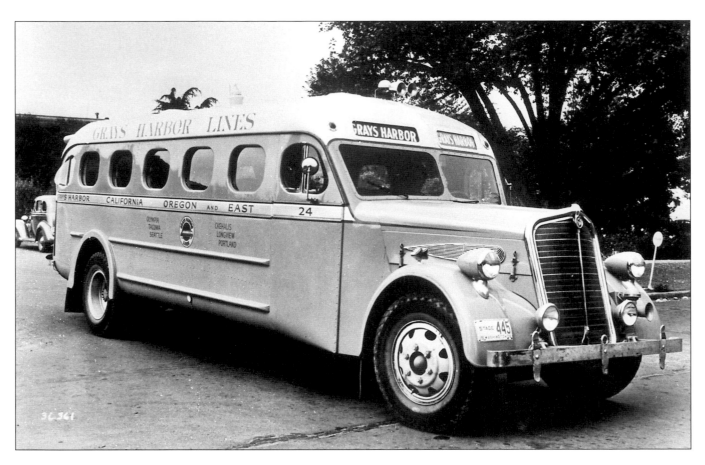

In 1936 Grays Harbor Lines, Aberdeen, Washington, bought two Model C-24 Kenworth buses, one of which is pictured here. These buses had Wentwin bodies. Kenworth didn't build bodies for buses, but depended on several bus body builders on the West Coast to complete the buses. Grays Harbor Lines operated a short route between Aberdeen and Olympia, Washington. *Motor Bus Society*

In the 1930s Kenworth built a number of deck-and-a-half style buses, most of which had under-floor engines. Washington Motor Coach System in Seattle acquired the deck-and-a-half Kenworth buses, but preferred front-engined designs like the one pictured here. This was one of six buses purchased in 1936. The Tricoach Corporation of Seattle built the bodies. Washington Motor Coach used these buses on its Seattle-Butte, Montana route, called the Northern Short Route.

A small bus company, Peoples Rapid Transit Company, Kalamazoo, Michigan, decided to build buses and introduced the Pony Cruiser in 1938. It was a lightweight 16-passenger bus with a Ford chassis. Later there were design changes, but after 13 years the company, then known as Kalamazoo Coaches, went out of business. Burlington Trailways bought a number of the Pony Cruisers for small feeder routes. This one and five others were acquired in late 1939.

The name "Clipper" came into the vocabulary of the bus industry in 1937 when The Flxible Company launched a new bus with the name Clipper. This was a 20-passenger bus mounted on a Chevrolet chassis. It had a full front with the engine inside to the right of the driver. Illinois Transit Line, Springfield, Illinois, was one of the early buyers of the new Clipper. Illinois Transit Line began in the mid-1930s with a main route between Davenport, Iowa and Terre Haute, Indiana via Springfield.

The Flxible Company of Loudonville, Ohio began selling a Chevrolet rear-engined Clipper bus in 1938. It accommodated 25 passengers and had a large baggage compartment in the rear. Queen City Coach Company of Charlotte, North Carolina was a good customer of Flxible buses. This bus was added to the Queen City fleet in 1938.

In October 1939 Airline Motor Coaches of Nacogdoches, Texas acquired this 29-passenger Buick rear-engined Flxible Clipper. The Flxible Company began building 29-passenger Clippers in 1939. Airline Motor Coaches was an important intercity bus company in East Texas.

New model buses were presented almost every year by the C. D. Beck & Co. after the company started in its Sidney, Ohio location in 1934. In 1939 the Steeliner was introduced. It was a small bus on a Chevrolet chassis. Red Ball Bus Company of Enid, Oklahoma featured this Beck in its fleet.

North Coast Lines, Seattle, Washington, bought the first ten Kenworth Model 610 buses in February 1939. These newly designed buses with bodies by the Pacific Coach & Foundry Company of Seattle were called Luxury Liners and saw service for a number of years on the Vancouver-Seattle-Portland route. North Coast bought ten more Model 620s the next year.

Four of these 1939 White Model 805M buses were the first new buses acquired for Acadian Coach Lines services in Nova Scotia from its base in Halifax. United Service Company started Acadian in 1938, and in 1955 it was sold to three Halifax individuals. White sold 102 Model 805M in three years with bodies on special orders from Bender Body Company. The Model 805M was similar to the White Model 706M.

Texas, New Mexico & Oklahoma (T.N.M. & O.) Coaches, Lubbock, Texas, originated in 1939 as a result of the merger of three regional bus companies in Texas. Two of the first T.N.M. & O. buses were these Kenworth Model 612 buses. They had bodies built by Wentworth and Irwin of Portland, Oregon. The bodies, seating 33 passengers, were called Roadliner bodies. Wentworth and Irwin, sometimes known as Wentwin, were building bodies for Kenworth buses as early as 1934. *Motor Bus Society*

Hayes Manufacturing Company (also known as Hayes-Anderson), Vancouver, British Columbia, was a large builder of trucks. The company also built some buses, including this Model PCT, built in 1938 for Central Canadian Greyhound Lines, which two years later became Western Canadian Greyhound Lines.

Western Auto and Truck Body Works of Winnipeg, Manitoba began building buses in the early 1930s. By 1939 the Western buses were referred to as Western Flyers. This bus for Manitoba Motor Transit, Ltd. of Brandon, Manitoba was one of the first of this type.

Streamlining and Diesel Power

Asignificant development for the bus industry was the introduction of the diesel engine. In 1932, Cummins Engine Company re-powered two buses, which were thought to be the first diesel-powered buses in the United States. Though Cummins developed the first diesel engine, no manufacturer used Cummins engines in great numbers until later in the century.

General Motors introduced its first diesel engine in the latter part of the 1930s. It was a two-cycle diesel engine rather than a four-cycle. The two-cycle engine provided adequate power and had long life, although it consumed more fuel than the four-cycle. However, this wasn't a great concern, as diesel fuel was not overly expensive and was in plentiful supply.

The General Motors engine had a niche that was very good for the bus industry, both intercity and city, but the intercity people really embraced the two-cycle engine. Other engine manufacturers such as Cummins and Caterpillar were continuing to improve their four-cycle diesel engines, but

The Model 743 Yellow Coach followed the successful Greyhound Model 719 bus in 1937. The two models were nearly identical, although the Model 743 had a number of refinements. Later deliveries of this bus model had diesel engines and also air conditioning.

concentrated on sales to the trucking industry. Although some General Motors engines were used on trucks, General Motors seemed to have a monopoly for the bus business. In fact, by the end of the 1930s the General Motors diesel engine became the primary engine in most Yellow Coach intercity and city buses.

General Motors was reluctant to allow any other companies to acquire its diesel engine because General Motors was also building buses. As a result, the General Motors diesel engines were said to be one of the factors causing a number of bus manufacturers to go out of business. Later, General Motors was required, under the settlement of an antitrust suit, to begin supplying its engine to other companies.

Greyhound Lines, with the cooperation of Yellow Coach, produced the Model 719 bus in 1936. It was one of the first intercity buses to mount the engine in the rear. Its high-level design, under-floor

The Greyhound Lines Model 743 bus, designed in conjunction with Yellow Coach, was purchased by selected other bus operators. Southern Limited, Inc., Chicago, Illinois, purchased six Model 743 Yellow Coach buses in 1938 for service on its routes south of Chicago.

Missouri Pacific Trailways of St. Louis, Missouri bought 27 Yellow Coach Model 1209 small buses in 1939. These 25-passenger buses were called Cruiserettes. Most bus manufacturers had small bus models to satisfy the needs of small operators. Missouri Pacific was a very large company but the Cruiserettes proved popular for branch lines.

baggage compartments and other features were considered innovations at that time. Though the coach was mainly for Greyhound, several other companies were allowed to acquire it and its successor, the Model 743. By the 1940s buses with engines in the rear were the most accepted designs, although buses with under-floor engines, such as the ACF buses, and front engines within the bodies, were also being manufactured.

In 1940 Greyhound introduced the "Silversides" coach. It was built by Yellow Coach and was known as the PGD 3751 and PDG 3751. The Silversides brought style and design to bus models. With its attractive, modern style, passengers looked at the new bus as being of the today age.

Pan American Bus Lines was formed in 1934 to operate a special through-bus service between New York City and Miami, Florida. In 1938 the company bought six 12-cylinder Model 7788 White buses for the service. The buses, one of which is pictured here, were based on White's transit-style body, but the intercity model had a sedan door and all forward-facing seats. Pan American had a checkered history and for a time was owned by Greyhound companies. *American Truck Historical Society*

The Union Pacific Railroad developed the famous Central Idaho winter resort, Sun Valley, in 1935. In 1939 this White Model 798 bus, with its interesting round windows, was acquired. It carried 26 passengers and had a large compartment in the rear to accommodate skis and baggage. A 12-cylinder flat engine powered the bus. *American Truck Historical Society*

This White Model 689 had a special streamlined body built by Bender Body Co. The Baltimore & Ohio Railroad had 30 of these buses and used them for train connecting service between Jersey City, New Jersey and New York City. Baltimore & Ohio contracted with Gray Line Motor Tours to provide the service. *American Truck Historical Society*

Canadian National Transportation Limited, a subsidiary of Canadian National Railways, operated bus systems in various parts of Canada. In Southern Ontario a sizable Canadian National operation existed. In 1940 two of these buses were bought from Brantford Coach and Body, Ltd. of Brantford, Ontario for that service. Brantford built only the body, which was mounted on a Leyland truck chassis shipped to Canada from England.

Eugene Prevost began building buses in 1924 in Ste. Claire, Quebec. Prior to World War II Prevost only built a few buses. Most of the early buses, like this 1940 model, were built on White or other truck chassis. The early buses produced by Prevost were acquired by some of the many small bus operators in Quebec.

International Transit, Ltd. of Port Arthur (now Thunder Bay), Ontario bought this bus in 1940. It had a Western Auto and Truck Body Works body. The chassis was built by Leyland in Britain and had a diesel engine. The bus accommodated 29 passengers.

B. C. Greyhound, Penticton, British Columbia, originally operated this bus, built by Hayes Manufacturing Company of Vancouver, British Columbia. When B. C. Greyhound became a part of Western Canadian Greyhound Lines in May 1944, this bus went into the Central Canadian Greyhound fleet. This bus was built in 1939 and was almost a duplicate of the Yellow Coach Models 719 and 743. However, this bus had an under-floor gasoline engine.

The Fitzjohn Coach Company introduced the 36-passenger Falcon Model 610 in 1940. It had an under-floor Hercules gasoline engine. DeLuxe Motor Stages of Illinois operated this Falcon on its Chicago-St. Louis main route, a service that began in 1930.

In 1940 Cincinnati & Lake Erie Bus System, Dayton, Ohio, bought five Superior Rocket buses, one of which is pictured here. The Superior Motor Coach Body Company got its start in 1923 in Lima, Ohio and changed its name to the Superior Coach Corporation in 1930. It is best known for school bus manufacture, but it did have transit bus and highway bus programs. Cincinnati & Lake Erie Bus System officially originated in 1930 and was sold to Great Lakes Greyhound Lines in 1947. *Motor Bus Society*

General American Aerocoach Company of Chicago acquired the bus building business of Gar Wood Industries in 1939. The 20-passenger Model PD, which is shown here, was a 1940 model with a Ford Mercury engine mounted in the rear. Fuller Bus Line of Bristol, Virginia, which operated four daily round trips between Bristol and Saltville, operated this bus. *Motor Bus Society*

Peoples Rapid Transit Company originated the Pony Cruiser bus in 1938. In 1940 a new management team was formed and the company became Kalamazoo Coaches in Kalamazoo, Michigan. A new bus design came in the early 1940s, and Stageways of Manitowoc, Wisconsin had one of the first new models. Stageways was a short-route bus line operating between Manitowoc and Appleton, Wisconsin.

Oregon Motor Stages in Portland operated several routes in northwestern Oregon. The company operated 51 Flx-ible Clipper buses between 1936 and 1944. This 29-passenger Buick-powered Clipper was one of them. The Flxible Company introduced this Clipper in 1940. It featured a number of changes over previous models, in particular the slanted, sliding-type passenger windows.

Dixie Coaches, Inc. of Tuscaloosa, Alabama operated this Beck Mainliner bus in 1941. It accommodated 33 pas-sengers and had an International Red Diamond engine. Dixie Coaches had a main route from Florence, Alabama through Tuscaloosa to Mobile, Alabama. Another route linked Birmingham with Florence.

The C. D. Beck & Co., Sidney, Ohio, offered the 33-passenger Luxury Liner bus from 1940 to 1942. It was available in 37-passenger and 33-passenger configurations. This 33-passenger Luxury Liner was a demonstrator with National Trailways Bus System livery to attract Trailways companies to buy this model Beck bus. International Red Diamond gasoline engines were used in the Luxury Liners.

The ACF 33 PB and 29 PB were smaller bus models introduced by ACF in 1940 for carriers that didn't require the larger 37-passenger buses. These models had Hall-Scott under-floor engines. Interurban Transportation Co., Alexandria, Louisiana, added five 29 PB ACF buses, like the one pictured here, in 1940.

Provincial Transport Company, Montreal, Quebec, bought this 29-passenger Yellow Coach Cruiserette Model PG 2902 in 1941, the year the PG 2902 was introduced. The Cruiserette model buses with G designations were powered by General Motors gasoline engines mounted in-line in the rear. Note the frost shield on the door window to allow the driver to see the mirror when winter weather deposited frost on the windows.

World War II and the Bus Industry

By 1940 intercity bus companies and bus manufacturers had, in most cases, overcome the difficult Depression years. However, it appeared there were new challenges ahead. World War II had begun, and although the United States was not initially involved, Canada was at war and the bus industry was affected with curtailments and shortages.

The United States felt a land route to the important Alaska Territory was a priority, and the Alaska Highway project became a focus of attention. Despite the many obstacles it presented, the Alaska Highway was completed in record time, and the bus industry was a vital contributor to its great success.

Although the Alaska Highway provided a route for trucks to carry vital supplies to the Alaskan outposts, passenger service was needed as well. A contract from the U.S. Corps of Engineers, North

In 1940 Greyhound Lines, in connection with Yellow Coach, introduced the Model PGG 3701 and PDG 3701 buses. They were called Silversides because of the stainless steel sides. They had high-deck seating and baggage storage below. The PGG models were gasoline powered and the PDG models were diesel powered. Greyhound and a few other selected companies received almost 500 prewar Silversides buses. The Silversides pictured was a 1941 Model PGG 3701 of Illinois Greyhound Lines. *Don Coffin collection*

West Service Command was awarded to Western Canadian Greyhound Lines to provide the vital passenger service. Twelve buses were built by the Fort Garry Body and Paint Works, Winnipeg, Manitoba, and dedicated to this service. They were a modern design with Hall-Scott under-floor gasoline engines. These buses traveled more than a million miles over the Alaska Highway without any incidents, and met many challenges, including steep hills, mountain grades, rivers to ford, and temperatures as low as -65 degrees Fahrenheit. Certainly the success was a tribute to the bus operation, the bus manufacturer, and to those who operated and maintained the buses.

Pictured is one of the 12 Fort Garry Auto and Truck Body Works buses assigned to the Northwest Service Command for service on the Alaska Highway when it was completed in 1942. These buses were noted for outstanding performance on the new highway under often-severe operating conditions and during extreme winter weather. Western Canadian Greyhound Lines was contracted for this service.

By the time the Alaska Highway was completed, the United States had entered World War II. Bus manufacturing stopped for a time, but the role of the bus industry became an important factor and some manufacturing resumed. Buses delivered during the war were stripped down, with no stainless steel trim, limited chrome, and drab, gray paint schemes. Some of these buses were quickly built school-type buses with high headroom bodies. They

Burlington Trailways, Chicago, Illinois, operated ten Yellow Coach PDG 3701 Silversides buses, acquiring them in 1941. These buses were diesel powered and air conditioned. The Silversides buses were almost exclusively for Greyhound companies, but other companies that had close relationships with Greyhound also bought them. Burlington Transportation Company began in 1929 as a subsidiary of the Chicago Burlington & Quincy Railroad Company. Burlington was a founding company of the National Trailways Bus System in 1936.

In 1941 The Flxible Company returned to building a front-engined bus along with its popular rear-engined Clippers. The new model was the 18-CF-41. It had a full front and a 235-cubic-inch Chevrolet six-cylinder engine. New Mexico Transportation Company, Roswell, New Mexico, added four of these 18-passenger Flxible buses in 1941. The first Flxible delivered to New Mexico Transportation Company was an Airway model in 1936. More Flxibles were added each year. Texas, New Mexico & Oklahoma (T.N.M. & O.) Coaches, Lubbock, Texas, acquired New Mexico Transportation Company in 1984.

In order to carry large numbers of defense workers during World War II, Santa Fe Trailways built this special 117-passenger bus in its Wichita, Kansas maintenance shop. It had a unique trailer arrangement with a motorized unit in front and the passengers seated on three levels. The bus was built mainly of plywood and called the Victory Liner. It was retired after World War II.

During World War II Carolina Trailways, Raleigh, North Carolina, which was in an area of several military establishments, transported many military passengers. To fill the demand for increased business, the company purchased a number of buses during the early 1940s, including this 1941 Aerocoach P-33. Ten more Aerocoach P-33 buses were added in 1942. Note that this bus was stripped of trimming; especially of chrome bumpers, because of wartime restrictions of certain metals.

were needed to move service men and women, and were vital in moving workers to and from munitions plants, which were located some distances from major metropolitan areas.

Fortunately, the great advances in technology in the late 1930s, particularly in the introduction of diesel engines and improved gasoline engines, helped buses perform admirably during the war. The bus industry received considerable praise for its contribution to the war effort. The persons involved in maintenance were commended for keeping the buses rolling, especially since some buses, which should have been retired, were kept

in service because of the limited production of new buses.

One part of the bus industry, the sightseeing service, was virtually closed down during the war years. Nevertheless, many sightseeing buses were utilized for important services for the duration of the war.

Wartime restrictions were imposed on buses, including reduced speeds to conserve fuel and tires. In spite of the restrictions, buses were able to keep a reasonably acceptable service. With the railroads unable to keep up with demand, the country was thankful for a healthy bus industry during World War II.

Southwestern Greyhound Lines, Fort Worth, Texas, added 20 Yellow Coach Model PDA 3701 buses to its fleet in 1942. The United States was involved in World War II at that time and wartime restrictions were in effect. However, because of the importance of transportation, Yellow Coach was allowed to build a limited number of buses. Greyhound ordered 328 of these buses for its operating companies.

This 1944 Yellow Coach PG 3701 was a wartime-built bus that didn't have chrome bumpers or other refinements but gave many companies like Oklahoma Transportation Company of Oklahoma City an opportunity to provide service to army installations and defense plants. Appropriately, this Oklahoma Transportation Company bus is pictured with a USO building in the background.

CHAPTER 6

Postwar Designs

Following World War II intercity bus companies began replacing many of their older buses that had worked hard during the war. While no new buses were introduced during the war years, bus manufacturers took advantage of the six years of the war to develop new designs, emphasizing a more modern look. Soon after the war ended many new buses were announced, and production of the new buses began soon afterward. Most postwar bus builders continued to produce intercity buses after the war, notably GM Truck & Coach Division (formerly Yellow Coach), ACF-Brill Motors (formerly ACF Motors), General American Aerocoach Co., Fitzjohn, Beck, and Flxible. There were a few newcomers in the intercity bus-building field as well.

In Fort William (now Thunder Bay), Ontario a war plant was quickly converted to build buses. The Canadian counterpart of ACF-Brill began building intercity and transit buses under the CCF-Brill

The Highway Division of the Bangor and Aroostook Railroad Company, Bangor, Maine, began in 1938 to operate buses between Bangor and Northern Maine. Bangor and Aroostook bought this GM PD 4104 bus in 1957. Five more PD 4104 buses were added later that year. The Highway Division discontinued bus service in 1984 after 46 years. The GM PD 4104 was a bus that had widespread popularity. Greyhound Lines had 1,981 of them in its fleet. Small companies like Bangor and Aroostook also found the bus important for their services.

Many bus companies began renewing their bus fleets soon after World War II. Greyhound Lines, Chicago, Illinois, placed an order for 1,500 PD 3751 Silversides buses from General Motors in 1947. The order totaled $37 million at that time. The PD 3751 buses were similar to the nearly 500 Yellow Coach Silversides buses built prior to World War II.

After World War II GM Truck & Coach Division continued to build the Cruiserette-style small bus. Pictured is one of the Cruiserette Model PG 2904 buses built with an open top and canvas covering, when not open. Utah Parks Company, Cedar City, Utah, took delivery of this bus in December 1946. It was one of the last open-top buses, which were once seen frequently in national parks.

name. Both ACF-Brill and CCF-Brill produced similar intercity, transit and trolley buses, making some changes from prewar models.

After the war Flxible introduced a 37-passenger model using two Chevrolet engines. Only 10 were built, reportedly because a fire at the factory destroyed the manufacturing equipment. That fire ended production of this new bus and Flxible concentrated on building smaller buses until 1955.

Many Trailways companies ordered a new postwar coach, the IC-41, from ACF-Brill Motors. These flagship buses had a Hall-Scott under-floor gasoline engine, though diesel eventually became available. Trailways companies used ACF-Brill coaches for a number of years, though they did not prove to be up to postwar trends. Some Greyhound Divisions also ordered ACF-Brill coaches, while some Trailways companies bought General Motors and other coaches. In its search for a flagship coach, Trailways looked for a short time to the Flxible Corporation, which offered a new, two-level bus that accommodated 37 passengers, had a Cummins diesel engine

GMC Truck and Coach Division of General Motors presented the new Model PD 4101 bus in 1948. It was a 41-passenger intercity bus with a 200-horsepower General Motors diesel engine mounted transversally in the rear. There were 335 Model PD 4101 buses built between 1948 and 1951. American Bus Lines, Chicago, Illinois, owned 25 of this model bus.

in the rear and Torsilastic® suspension. However, this vehicle didn't fill Trailways' need for a flagship coach and Trailways looked to other makes.

By the early 1950s almost every bus sold by GM Truck & Coach Division had the General Motors diesel engine. Manufacturers of buses still using gasoline engines could not compete with the General Motors diesel. By 1953 the Twin Coach Company and ACF-Brill closed their doors and White Motor Company discontinued bus production. Among the other companies discontinuing intercity bus production were Aerocoach, Beck and Fitzjohn.

In 1948 the Allison Transmission Division of General Motors introduced the Power Shift Transmission, but this was primarily for city buses. It did not find usage for intercity buses. Automatic transmissions were later developed for the intercity bus.

A new era for the bus business began in 1953 when General Motors introduced air suspension, a real breakthrough in bus technology. Prior to that time leaf springs were used on buses. Air suspension

Asbury Park-New York Transit Company of Asbury Park, New Jersey was formed in 1929, operating between Asbury Park and New York City. In 1951, the company added four GM PD 4103 buses. The PD 4103 succeeded the PD 4102, which was built in limited numbers. Both the PD 4102 and the PD 4103 had a newly styled front but a body similar to the PD 4101 model by General Motors.

In 1946 Kaiser Industries of Permanente, California built this one-of-a-kind articulated bus. It was 60 feet long and had a six-cylinder Cummins diesel engine located under the front floor. It was operated until 1951, first by Santa Fe Trailways and then by Continental Trailways when Santa Fe Trailways became a part of Continental. Kaiser Industries built no other buses.

This bus was built by CCF-Brill (Canadian Car & Foundry Co.) of Fort William (now Thunder Bay), Ontario in 1946. It was one of 22 Model IC-41 CCF-Brill buses acquired by Pacific Stage Lines, Vancouver, British Columbia, and the first bus of that type sold to a Canadian company. Another 36 of the IC-41 buses were added to the Pacific Stage Lines fleet the next year. After operating in intercity service in the Vancouver area, this bus later went into sightseeing service. The Model IC-41 had a Hall-Scott under-floor engine and was similar to the Model IC-41 bus built by ACF-Brill in Philadelphia, Pennsylvania. Approximately 300 of the CCF-Brill IC-41s were built in Canada.

provided a more comfortable, level ride. In addition, leaf springs required more maintenance, while air suspension was, and still is, almost maintenance free, a real plus. General Motors PD 4104 model, introduced in 1953, featured the new air suspension. Its much improved ride encouraged many intercity bus companies, both large and small, to add the bus to their fleets. Torsilastic suspension also was introduced after the war, but air suspension became the more popular system. However, some bus companies continued to use Torsilastic suspensions for a number of years.

Several companies built deck-and-a-half buses in the 1920s and 1930s. The innovative design was especially common in the west. Deck-and-a-half buses attracted passengers by offering them a better view for sightseeing. In addition, there was more opportunity for storing baggage in the space below the top passenger deck. Deck-and-a-half buses lost their favor in the mid-1930s. The design came back into use after Greyhound introduced its very popular Scenicruiser in 1954. The Scenicruiser was a 40-foot, 47-passenger bus with tandem rear

The Twin Coach Co., Kent, Ohio, tried to introduce a new intercity bus after World War II. The Model 360 was built in 1947. It had two engines, Torsilastic suspension, air conditioning and numerous passenger amenities. One prototype was built. American Bus Lines operated this one-of-a-kind bus with a vision to order a large fleet of the buses for luxury transcontinental service. However, the Model 360 Twin Coach did not meet with success. American Buslines met with a lack of financing, and this put an end to a fleet of intercity buses built by the Twin Coach Company.

axles, two diesel engines, and a lavatory. Designed by Greyhound and General Motors, 1,001 of the buses were built exclusively for Greyhound. This bus had passenger appeal and helped Greyhound attract more business in the postwar years. Eventually a single V-8 diesel engine replaced the two diesel engines. Many companies copied the deck-and-a-half design, including Beck, Flxible and Western Flyer.

After World War II, sightseeing became even more popular for the bus industry. Several manufacturers began building glass-top buses. Western Flyer was one of the first companies to offer glass-top buses. Others followed almost immediately and in later years.

Kaiser Industries built a single coach, a luxury articulated model, which was operated by Santa Fe Trailways. It was the first large articulated intercity bus, but the concept never caught on. It just didn't seem to be appropriate at the time. Unlike in Europe, bus companies in the United States never developed an interest in articulated intercity buses. Even articulated city buses did not find favor until later years.

In an attempt to introduce a special bus with a new appearance in the post-World War II years, Continental Trailways, Dallas, Texas, had this prototype deck-and-a-half bus built by ACF-Brill Motors of Philadelphia, Pennsylvania. It had many passenger amenities, including a buffet and lavatory. A Hall-Scott 267-horsepower gasoline engine was used. The bus didn't prove successful and only one was built.

ACF Motors in Philadelphia, Pennsylvania became ACF-Brill Motors Co. after World War II. Its intercity bus design was changed very little except for the appearance of the front. It used the same under-floor Hall-Scott gasoline engine used in previous models. Diesel engines were becoming the engine of choice by the bus industry, and in 1951 some design changes and a Cummins diesel engine were made available in the ACF-Brill intercity bus. Two years later, all ACF-Brill bus production ended. Pictured is one of the last ACF-Brill intercity buses. Continental Dixie Lines of Dallas, Texas operated it.

This 1946 Chevrolet sedan bus was the pride of the Roswell-Carrizozo Stage Line, a small bus company that operated in Central New Mexico. It is shown in January 1948 stopped in Tinnie, New Mexico at the Tinnie Mercantile Company, which was the local bus stop in that small town. Note the partial covering of the grille, called a winter front, used to keep the engine warm in the cold mountain weather.

Jefferson Transportation Company, Minneapolis, Minnesota, inaugurated a special limousine service between Minneapolis and Rochester, Minnesota soon after World War II. Two special-built Cadillac sedans were used. They each accommodated seven passengers. This service carried passengers who traveled by train to the Mayo Clinic and to hospitals in the Rochester area. Rochester did not have connecting rail service at that time. Larger stretched Mercury and Chrysler sedans were later used.

Spartan Coach & Manufacturing Co., Sturgis, Michigan, was in business only three years. It began in 1946 by building 21-passenger buses constructed with welded steel tubing and aluminum alloy panels. An International Blue Diamond engine mounted in-line in the rear powered the original models. Larger models were introduced later. The demand for small buses waned and Spartan eventually went out of business. Sun Valley Stages of Twin Falls, Idaho operated one of the 21-passenger Spartans.

Crown Coach Corporation of Los Angeles, a school bus and fire truck builder, expanded its production in the early 1950s to build intercity and sightseeing buses. This 33-passenger bus went into service for Nava-Hopi Tours, Flagstaff, Arizona, around 1952. Nava-Hopi Tours, which began in 1928, operated sightseeing trips to the Grand Canyon and also had some regular route service as well as charter and tour services. It was a member of the Gray Line Sightseeing Association. It ceased operations in 2002.

Tanner Motor Tours of Los Angeles was one of the largest companies in the Gray Line Sightseeing Association, and at one time had 150 buses. Crown Body & Coach Corporation of Los Angeles built a number of the Tanner buses. Crown had its beginnings early in the 20th century but didn't get involved in buses until 1933, when its first school bus was built. The bus pictured here was a 1946 Crown sightseeing bus for Tanner. A Hall-Scott under-floor gasoline engine powered it.

Intermountain Transportation Company, Anaconda, Montana, had five of these Model W-1 Kenworth intercity buses, the first acquired in 1947. Kenworth built only 25 of these Model W-1 buses. Hall-Scott under-floor engines powered them. Intermountain began in 1917 and had a number of routes in Montana. After more than 75 years it closed its operations and Rimrock Stages of Billings, Montana assumed most of its routes.

Indiana Railroad, Indianapolis, Indiana, began as an interurban railroad in the later part of the 19th century under another name. Indiana Railroad had a sizable interurban system, but in the mid-1930s, because of high costs and the Depression, began substituting its electric rail routes with bus services and became a full bus company in 1941. Indiana Railroad became a part of the Wesson Company and following World War II it operated 50 37-passenger Aerocoach buses like the one pictured here.

Monumental Motor Tours, Baltimore, Maryland, was one of the oldest bus companies dedicated to charter and tour service, beginning in 1925. Monumental began acquiring Aerocoach buses in 1942. This Aerocoach Model P-46 37 joined the Monumental fleet with 18 others in 1947. The General American Aerocoach Company, Chicago, Illinois, began building buses in 1940 when it took over Gar Wood Industries. The Model P-46 37 Aerocoaches featured rear-mounted International Red Diamond gasoline engines.

The Model P-372 Aerocoach was almost the same as the Mastercraft series buses introduced in 1940. The new Model 372 had a newly styled front and silver siding. It was first presented in 1949. Pacific Trailways, Bend, Oregon, operated an important Trailways route between Portland, Oregon and Salt Lake City, Utah and had seven of these Aerocoach buses. The one pictured here was purchased in 1950. It had a Continental gasoline engine. The General American Aerocoach Company of Chicago, builder of Aerocoach buses, went out of business in 1952.

The Flxible Company of Loudonville, Ohio continued to build the Clipper bus after World War II. The postwar Clippers were very similar to the prewar models except that by late 1946 the front had been made more rounded with only one bumper instead of three as seen in the earlier Clippers. Acadian Lines, Halifax, Nova Scotia, was a good Flxible customer, and ordered several of the new Clippers that were delivered in 1947.

The Flxible Company, Loudonville, Ohio, introduced a new 37-passenger intercity bus, the Model C-1, in 1948. This new Flxible Clipper had two Chevrolet engines. It did not prove successful, and only eight were built. The State College of Iowa, Cedar Falls, bought one of the eight in 1950. Many other Flxible intercity buses were acquired by colleges and universities to transport athletic teams and students on field trips.

The Flxible Company, Loudonville, Ohio, introduced the Visicoach 29-passenger bus in 1950. It followed the same lines as the Clipper models produced for a decade previously. The major difference was the elongated, slanted sliding windows on the side. Jack Rabbit Lines, Sioux Falls, South Dakota, which purchased Flxible buses for a number of years, added this Visicoach and one other in 1950. Jack Rabbit Lines began in 1924 and served much of South Dakota, and also provided some service into North Dakota and Minnesota.

This Fitzjohn Falcon Model 610 was one of 12 buses delivered to All American Bus Lines, Chicago, Illinois, in 1945. All American previously bought 35 Fitzjohn Model 610 Falcon buses. All American had a slow start in its transcontinental service, which began in 1935, and used a variety of small buses, mainly Fords. The company grew to be a large transcontinental carrier by the time these buses were added to the fleet.

The Fitzjohn Model 510 Duraliner was one of the most popular intercity buses built by the Fitzjohn Coach Co. of Muskegon, Michigan. It had a Hercules engine mounted inside at the front of the bus. The first post-World War II Duraliner was introduced in 1946. This Duraliner was operated by River Trails Transit Lines of Galena, Illinois, a company with some intercity services but primarily in school bus services and charters and tours. A number of Duraliners were sold to operators in Canada.

Fitzjohn Coach Company, Muskegon, Michigan, had built front-engined intercity buses for many years, even in the postwar era. In order to stay competitive, a new 37-passenger, rear-engined intercity bus, the Roadrunner, was introduced in 1954. Cummins JBS diesel engines were standard. Demand for the Roadrunner was weak. Some were sold to Trailways companies and a number went to Canada. Chatham (Ontario) Coach Lines operated this 1955 Roadrunner on its intercity services and charters in Southern Ontario. It originally had a Waukesha 140-OK engine, but the engine was later changed to a Cummins. Fitzjohn Coach Company closed its doors in 1958 after almost 40 years in the bus industry.

In 1946 Motor Coach Industries (MCI), Winnipeg, Manitoba, introduced its first rear-engined bus, the Courier 100. This bus had an International RD 450 engine and incorporated a number of changes from previous MCI models. Eagle Bus Lines, Winnipeg, Manitoba, bought this MCI Courier 100 in 1946. Eagle Bus Lines, which had its roots traced to the mid-1930s, operated suburban service northeast of Winnipeg. Beaver Bus Line acquired it in 1990.

This 1948 Prevost Model I-29 Interurban bus was operated by Autobus LacFrontiere, Ltd., Quebec City, Quebec, which had a route between Quebec City and Lac-Frontiere on the Quebec-Maine border. The company sold to Transport Fontaine in 1977. Most Prevost Interurban model buses had the front axle behind the entrance door. This particular model had the entrance door behind the front axle. A Ford 317-horsepower engine was used.

Following World War II the Prevost company, Ste. Claire, Quebec, took advantage of the demand for new buses and introduced the Interurban models, rear-engined buses seating 29 to 37 passengers. Although sold mainly in Eastern Canada, they were marketed throughout Canada. This 1947 Prevost Interurban was in the Autobus DesMarais, Limited fleet, which operated out of Joliette, Quebec. The company began in 1937 and was sold to Autobus Gaudreault Enrg. in 1963.

Transport Fontaine, Ltee., St-Gervais, Quebec, purchased this Prevost Interurban Model I-33 bus in 1950, two years after the company was incorporated. Transport Fontaine was a small bus company operating an intercity route southeast of Quebec City. The Prevost Interurban model was a new postwar design. An International Red Diamond engine mounted in the rear was standard.

Canadian Coachways, Edmonton, Alberta, not only had an important passenger business in Northern Alberta and British Columbia, but also carried considerable freight on its regular scheduled routes. To accommodate this type of business, the company operated a number of vehicles called Brucks, a combination bus and truck. This Bruck was a 1947 Western Flyer Model T-32, purchased secondhand from Thiessen Transportation Co. and converted to a Bruck by Coachways.

After World War II, Western Flyer Coach Company continued to build front-engined body-on-chassis buses. They proved popular among many bus operators throughout Canada, especially on routes without paved highways. Canadian National Transportation, Limited bought three of the T-36/40 Western Flyers in 1953 for train connecting service between Kamsack, Saskatchewan and the mining town of Flin Flon, Manitoba.

After building front-engined buses for almost 20 years, Western Flyer Coach, Ltd. (formerly Western Auto and Truck Body Works), Winnipeg, Manitoba, introduced the new rear-engined Western Flyer Canuck in 1953. It was a 33-passenger bus with an International Red Diamond gasoline engine. A Cummins diesel engine was an option. Pictured here is the prototype, which was operated by Moore's Taxi of Winnipeg, Manitoba. Later models were modified.

The Canadian Car and Foundry Co. (CCF-Brill), Fort William (now Thunder Bay), Ontario, began producing the Voyageur Model ICW-29 buses in 1952. The Voyageur was a 29-passenger bus powered with a rear-mounted British AEC six-cylinder diesel engine. Beaver Bus Lines, Winnipeg, Manitoba, had two of these Voyageur buses that the company operated on its Winnipeg-Selkirk, Manitoba route. Beaver Bus Lines began in 1940 and acquired the Winnipeg-Selkirk route from the Winnipeg Electric Company after World War II.

Toye Brothers, New Orleans, Louisiana, was a Gray Line Sightseeing company in the New Orleans area. In addition to a fleet of ACF-Brill sightseeing buses, this Beck bus was in its fleet. This was a front-engined Beck Super Steeliner Model 400 bus. Beck built these buses between 1948 and 1951. Toye Brothers celebrated its 100th anniversary in 1952.

Kerrville Bus Company, Kerrville, Texas, was one of the owners of the 12 DH 1000 series deck-and-a-half model Beck buses, which were presented in 1950. The Beck DH 1000, which was ahead of most of the post-World War II deck-and-a-half buses, had a tandem rear axle and a Cummins NHRBS diesel engine. Kerrville was a good customer of Beck buses and was also a distributor. Kerrville has an extensive route network in Texas centered in the Austin, Houston and San Antonio areas.

Model 9200 buses were built by the C. D. Beck & Co. between 1954 and 1957. A glass-top sightseeing-type bus called the Skyliner, like this one pictured for Gray Line in Chicago, was one of the 36 buses built in this series. The Skyliner and similar Model 9200 buses had air suspension and Cummins diesel engines.

The Scenicruiser was an effort by the Greyhound Corporation to promote bus travel in the 1950s. It was a deck-and-a-half model, 40-feet long and with a tandem rear axle. General Motors began building these buses in 1954 and designated them the PD 4501 model. There were 1,001 Scenicruisers built. Original models had two General Motors 4-71 diesel engines but this did not prove satisfactory. After General Motors introduced the 8V-71 diesel engine, the Scenicruisers were re-powered with the more powerful single engine.

One of the many bus models built by the C. D. Beck & Co. was the Model 9600 series. It had a modified deck-and-a-half design. First presented in 1956, it was produced for only one year. Only 17 were built. Queen City Trailways, Charlotte, North Carolina, a pioneer bus company in the Carolinas, operated this Beck 9600. The Model 9600 was the last bus to have the Beck name. Mack Trucks took over the Beck plant in Sidney, Ohio in 1958, and after that the buses built there featured the Mack name.

In 1953 GM Truck and Coach Division of General Motors presented the Model PD 4104 bus. This newly designed intercity bus had many innovations, the most significant being air suspension. The air suspension system gave superior ride quality and also required a minimum of maintenance. Air conditioning powered by a small gasoline engine was standard in most PD 4104 buses. Vermont Transit Lines, Burlington, Vermont, a pioneer New England bus company beginning in 1929, operated 25 GM PD 4104 buses. The PD 4104 pictured here is one of three acquired in 1953.

This GM Model PD 4104 was one of 15 buses purchased by Public Service Coordinated Transport, Newark, New Jersey, in 1953. It accommodated 41 passengers and had roof windows for sightseeing. It was one of the most successful intercity buses, with 5,065 built between 1953 and 1960. This model was the most popular intercity bus at that time. A General Motors 6-71 diesel engine was mounted transversally at the rear of the bus.

Limited access highways, including turnpikes, were being constructed in the late 1940s and 1950s preceding the Federal Aid Highway Act in 1956, which introduced the Interstate Highway System. This gave bus companies an opportunity to offer better service to many communities. Pictured here, just leaving the New Jersey Turnpike, is a 1954 GM PD 4104 bus owned by Quaker City Lines, Philadelphia, Pennsylvania. This was one of six of the 45-passenger models purchased by Quaker City in 1954. Three more were added in 1955.

The first intercity buses to carry the GM nameplate, instead of the Yellow Coach nameplate, were Model PDA 3702 and PGA 3702 buses, which were built in the GMC Truck and Coach plant in Pontiac, Michigan in 1944. The Model PDA 3703 followed these models in 1947. Checkerway Charter Coach Company of Chicago became the owner of this GMC PDA 3703 in July 1949. Checkerway was one of a number of charter bus companies that became quite an important market for buses following World War II.

This Greyhound bus was one of a kind. It was built in 1957 by Mack Trucks, Allentown, Pennsylvania, and was operated for an evaluation by Greyhound between Chicago and Los Angeles in 1958. Originally this 39-passenger, 40-foot bus had a Mack ENDT-674 engine. This Mack Model MV6200 was an attempt by Mack to win orders from Greyhound, but Greyhound officials didn't feel the bus fit their program for a new-style bus and it was returned to Mack.

In 1955 Queen City Trailways, Charlotte, North Carolina, purchased four of these three-axle, 40-foot deck-and-a-half buses from the C. D. Beck & Co. These large buses seated 47 passengers, had Cummins NHRVS600 diesel engines mounted in the rear and were air-conditioned. Only 12 were built. Cuban bus companies acquired seven.

When the Straits of Mackinac Bridge, a five-mile structure with a central suspension section, was completed in 1957, Blue Bird intercity buses were operated by the Bridge Authority between St. Ignace on Michigan's Upper Peninsula and Mackinaw City at the top of the Upper Peninsula. The Authority operated two of these buses over the bridge until 1970, at which time an on-call service was initiated.

In 1932 Northern Transportation Company began operating bus service from its base in Bemidji, Minnesota to International Falls on the Canadian border. Three years later a line between Virginia, Minnesota and International Falls was added. In 1958 the company acquired this Flxible Starliner bus. The Starliner model was launched in 1957. It was the last Clipper-style, 29-passenger bus built by The Flxible Company.

The Vista Liner Model 228JT1 was a deck-and-a-half bus built by The Flxible Company and introduced in 1955. A Cummins diesel engine was mounted in-line in the rear. Trailways companies bought a number of the Vista Liners, but it did not prove to be the answer to Trailways for a new flagship bus for its long-distance services. Only 228 were built.

The Flxible Company, Loudonville, Ohio, introduced the Hi-Level model in 1960. It featured a roofline that extended almost to the front of the bus. The driver sat at a lower level. A Detroit Diesel 6V-71 diesel engine was used. Triangle Transportation Company of East Grand Forks, Minnesota operated this Flxible Hi-Level bus in the 1960s. Triangle Transportation was a pioneer Minnesota bus company having its start in 1921.

The last intercity bus model produced by The Flxible Company was presented in 1964. Called the Flxiliner, it was 35 feet long, and normally accommodated 37 passengers. A Detroit Diesel 6V-71 diesel engine powered the Flxiliner. A total of 233 were built. The Flxible Company ended its many years of building intercity buses in 1970, and then concentrated its efforts on transit buses.

Survival Buses

Automobile production reached all-time highs following World War II. Intercity bus companies saw a decrease in passenger totals as people began using their new automobiles for traveling instead of using buses or other modes of transportation. To combat this, bus companies began to place more emphasis on charter and tour services. Carrying packages also helped intercity bus companies.

New highway building was a boon to long-distance bus travel, with several turnpikes opening. In 1956 President Dwight D. Eisenhower signed the Federal Aid Highway Act, which launched the construction of the Interstate Highway System. The highway system allowed bus travel to compete with the schedule of many train services and made bus travel more convenient.

Completion of all segments of the Trans-Canada Highway contributed to considerable activity in long-distance bus service in Canada, allowing Greyhound Canada to operate through-services between eastern and western Canada.

This Motor Coach Industries Courier Model 96-D bus was added to the fleet of Abitibi Coach Lines of Val d'Or, Quebec in 1957. The company was founded in 1931 and operated routes mainly in the Northwestern part of Quebec and a long route from that area to Montreal. Provincial Transport Enterprises acquired the company in the early 1960s. The Model 96-D had 41 seats, air suspension and a General Motors 4-71 diesel engine.

The Motor Coach Industries Courier 96 Model was produced beginning in 1957. It had a 35-foot body and seating for 41 passengers. A General Motors 4-71 diesel engine was mounted in the rear. The Courier 96 also featured air suspension. Greyhound Canada had 29 of these buses in its fleet, acquiring all of them in 1957. This Courier 96 was pictured while en route between Sault Ste. Marie and North Bay, Ontario.

A number of manufacturers built deck-and-a-half buses after Greyhound introduced the Scenicruiser in 1954. Western Flyer Coach, Ltd. of Winnipeg, Manitoba built four deck-and-a-half models, which were powered by International Red Diamond engines mounted in the front. Thiessen Transportation Co., Steinbach, Manitoba, bought two of these Model T36-40 2L buses. Thiessen began in 1946 and eventually bought out a number of Manitoba bus companies, including Grey Goose Bus Line. The expanded bus operation adopted the Grey Goose name. In 1963 the owners of Grey Goose, including A. J. Thiessen, founder of Thiessen Transportation, acquired Western Flyer Coach.

By the mid-1950s most of the manufacturers of postwar intercity buses had gone by the wayside. The only manufacturers left in the United States were essentially General Motors and Flxible. A good deal of that was because of the General Motors diesel engine. Others just couldn't compete with the General Motors exclusive. After the settlement of an antitrust suit, General Motors was required to allow its diesel engine to be purchased by other bus builders. Flxible discontinued making intercity buses by the end of the 1960s.

Canadian bus manufacturers managed to survive better during the 1950s than many of their counterparts in the United States. Motor Coach Industries, Western Flyer Limited and Prevost continued to build buses in Canada. Western Auto & Truck Body in Winnipeg had been building the front-engined Flyer, and in 1955 introduced a new rear-engined bus, the Canuck.

General Motors developed an eight-cylinder diesel engine late in 1959. The first bus with a V-8 engine was the PD 4106, introduced by GM Truck & Coach Division in 1961. The V-8 engine became the standard for large buses for many years. The more powerful V-8 diesel engine eliminated the need for a separate engine heretofore necessary to power the air conditioning system. A later GM model, the PD 4107, had an interesting step-up seating configuration in the front. Most of these buses had on-board lavatories.

Trailways went to Ulm, Germany in search of a competitor for Greyhound's Scenicruiser. The Karl Kassbohrer bus-building firm produced a new 40-foot, three-axle coach named the Golden Eagle for Continental Trailways. Continental found the Eagle-style coaches to be a good fit and standardized on them. Continental eventually set up a plant in Belgium to build the coaches, which were then referred to as Silver Eagles. Eventually, manufacturing for the Eagle buses was brought to the United States with a new plant in Brownsville, Texas, where Eagle buses were built for a number of years.

Earlier, Continental Trailways acquired eight articulated buses from the Kassbohrer firm. Four were Golden Eagle designs, and four, called Academy Express buses, were European styles. Even with the introduction of these buses the interest in intercity articulated buses did not last and there were none built for some time.

In 1958 Greyhound Lines of Canada, which had a previous interest in Motor Coach Industries (MCI), acquired full ownership. The company was building the rear-engined Courier Model 100 for Greyhound, as well as for other Canadian companies, in its plant in Winnipeg. In April 1962 MCI opened an assembly plant across the U.S. border in Pembina, North Dakota. Bus body shells were trucked to Pembina for final assembly. In 1963 MCI buses were built for Greyhound Lines in the United States. The new Model MC-5 was also offered for sale to all bus companies.

Prevost, which built a limited number of buses, mainly for eastern Canada, accelerated its building program and began marketing buses throughout all of Canada.

Moose Mountain Lines, Regina, Saskatchewan, began in 1955. It was formed to take over some routes in Southeastern Saskatchewan that had been eliminated by Saskatchewan Transportation Company. Moose Mountain Lines changed hands several times, and in 1994 the owners of Beaver Bus Lines of Winnipeg, Manitoba acquired it. Moose Mountain Lines purchased this Western Flyer Canuck Model P-41R in 1960. The Western Flyer Canuck was first introduced in 1953, and then was slightly redesigned in 1957. A larger model Canuck, the P-41, came in 1958. The General Motors 6V-71 became the standard engine for the Canuck.

Canadian Coachways was a large intercity bus company serving areas in Northern Alberta and British Columbia, as well as Northwest Territories and Yukon. The company had its beginnings in 1929 and expanded by acquiring smaller bus companies and pioneering new routes. Canadian Coachways was a good customer of Western Flyer Coach. In 1965 Western changed the appearance of the Model 500 with full "silversiding" and different side windows. Canadian Coachways acquired the prototype Western Model 500 pictured here. Greyhound Lines of Canada purchased Canadian Coachways in 1969.

The Western Flyer Model 600 was first built in 1967 and was followed by the Model 600A in 1968. It was an unusual bus because it was 38 feet long and had only two axles. In most jurisdictions a bus longer than 35 feet required a third axle. All Model 600s and 600As were sold to Canadian operators in areas where the longer buses were allowed. Grey Goose Bus Lines, Winnipeg, Manitoba, had this Model 600 and 12 others. These buses had Detroit Diesel 8V-71 diesel engines. The Model 600As were the last intercity buses built by Western Flyer Coach.

The Golden Eagle was the name Continental Trailways gave to this bus, which was built by Karl Kassbohrer, AG, in Stuttgart, Germany. Continental was looking for a new luxury bus for long-distance services and chose this model. Golden Eagle Five Star services were established for various routes. The Five Star services featured hostesses, snacks and other passenger enhancements. Continental acquired 51 of the Golden Eagle buses from Germany in 1956 and 1957.

The Silver Eagle followed the Golden Eagle into the Continental Trailways fleet. Karl Kassbohrer, AG, built the original 41 Silver Eagles in Stuttgart, Germany. Continental Trailways found the Eagle design quite successful and when Kassbohrer could not continue building Eagles, Continental established a plant in Brugge, Belgium to build the Eagle buses. The Kass-bohrer Silver Eagles were built from 1956 to 1959 and Belgian Silver Eagles from 1960. Pictured is the first Silver Eagle model.

Although the Silver Eagle was a bus built by Continental Trailways and used almost exclusively on Continental Trailways' routes, it was made available to other bus operators. It was built first in Germany in 1958, and then in Belgium until 1968, when production was moved to Brownsville, Texas. The Silver Eagle was a 47-passenger, three-axle bus.

Continental Rocky Mountain Lines, Denver, Colorado, imported two articulated buses in 1957 from Karl Kassbohrer, AG, in Stuttgart, Germany. They were operated on the heavily trafficked route between Denver and Pueblo, Colorado via Colorado Springs where the United States Air Force Academy is located. Hence, the name Academy Express was used. The buses featured Cummins under-floor diesel engines.

In 1958, four articulated Golden Eagle buses were acquired by Continental Trailways from Karl Kassbohrer, AG, in Stuttgart, Germany. Two articulated Kassbohrer buses had been used on the Denver-Colorado Springs-Pueblo route but they did not prove satisfactory, and the Eagle-designed articulated model was substituted. They had air conditioning and under-floor baggage space, which was not available on the previous articulated buses. The larger Golden Eagle articulated buses were removed from that service and operated in California until 1965.

General Motors Corporation had a presence in Canada operating a manufacturing facility beginning in 1948. In 1961 the plant in London, Ontario began building GM New Look transit buses. Pictured is a GM SDM 4501 built in 1962 for Charterways Transportation, Limited of London, Ontario. This bus design was similar to transit and suburban buses built at that time. Some intercity companies chose to buy this suburban bus for intercity routes.

White River Coach Lines, White River Junction, Vermont, was one of the many small bus companies that purchased GM PD 4106 buses. The White River GM PD 4106 pictured here was purchased in 1964. The appearance of the PD 4106 was slightly different than the successful Model PD 4104. The side windows were larger and there were changes to the front and back of the bus. White River Coach Lines had its start in 1939 as Twin State Transportation Co. It sold to Vermont Transit Lines in 1967.

In 1961 the Greyhound Scenicruiser was a familiar sight along highways throughout the United States. At that time Greyhound decided to give the Scenicruiser a new look. The lettering was changed to read "Greyhound" in large, bold letters, and a gold stripe was added around the body. At the same time, the Scenicruiser's two engines were replaced by a single General Motors 8V-71 diesel engine.

This General Motors Model PD 4106 was one of two that were delivered to Ohio Bus Line Co., Cincinnati, in 1965. Ohio Bus Line Co. was a subsidiary of the Cincinnati Transit Company, and operated a route serving Cincinnati and Dayton, Ohio, and Richmond, Indiana. The company began in 1925 and closed its doors in 1972. Many companies, large and small, acquired the Model PD 4106. Between 1961 and 1965 a total of 3,226 PD 4106 buses were built.

The General Motors Model PD 4106 bus was introduced in 1961. The appearance of this new bus and the previous Model PD 4104 was quite similar, although there were larger side windows and changes in both the front and rear styling. This new GM model had a larger General Motors 8V-71 diesel engine. It had greater power and the air conditioning system could be run from the main engine. The Arrow Line, Hartford, Connecticut, bought this PD 4106 in 1965. The Arrow Line began in 1929 and served a route between Albany, New York and Hartford, Connecticut. It has also been very involved in charters and tours.

In 1968, Prevost Car, Inc., Ste. Claire, Quebec, introduced the Champion TS 4776 model. It was the first Prevost bus to be marketed in the United States. In 1968, Somerset Bus Company, Mountainside, New Jersey, was the first bus company in the United States to take delivery of Prevost Champion buses. Four were added to the company's fleet at that time. Detroit Diesel 8V-71 diesel engines powered the Champions.

Motor Coach Industries (MCI), Winnipeg, Manitoba, began building a new style bus in 1958. It was known as the Model MC-1. It was followed, with the same basic body style, by the MC-2, MC-3, and MC-4. One of the MC-4 buses is pictured here. Greyhound Lines of Canada, Calgary, Alberta, bought 16 MC-4 buses in 1963. This bus was labeled Trans Canada Highway Tours, for Greyhound Lines of Canada's tour program. The new MCI buses had air suspension, and the MC-4 was the first to have a General Motors 8V-71 diesel engine.

SMT (Eastern), Limited, Moncton, New Brunswick, is a bus company which has been serving most of the Province of New Brunswick since 1938. The company has been a good customer of Motor Coach Industries (MCI) buses. Pictured here is a 1964 MCI Model MCC-5, one of six delivered that year. The MCI Model MCC for Canada and the Model MCA for the United States were only built for two years, but 300 units were produced in total.

New Technology and New Rules

Throughout the history of the industry, bus manufacturers continually developed larger buses with increased seating capacities. Almost all intercity buses sold in the United States were diesel powered and General Motors produced almost all of the engines. The name of General Motors' diesel division was changed to Detroit Diesel Division in 1965. Later the Detroit Diesel and Allison Divisions of General Motors merged to form Detroit Diesel Allison Division.

When Motor Coach Industries (MCI) began producing its first 40-foot bus, the 96-inch-wide MC-7, in 1968, it marked a crucial date for the industry. There had been 40-foot buses prior to that time that proved very successful, and the industry trend was definitely leaning toward 40-foot buses, but 1968 marked the beginning of the 40-foot bus as the industry standard. The demand was strong for 40-foot buses, and many companies in the U.S.

In 1967 Greyhound Lines had a new prototype bus built by Motor Coach Industries, known as the Model MC-6. These buses were an exclusive Greyhound bus in an attempt to have a more modern bus to replace the aging Scenicruiser models, which were also a Greyhound exclusive. The MC-6 was 102 inches wide. The new width had not been authorized for buses in most states, and it wasn't until 1985 that 102-inch buses were legalized almost everywhere. The first MC-6 models had the rear tag axle wheels covered.

Following the completion of two prototype Motor Coach Industries Model MC-6 buses, 98 more were built in 1968. There were 15 MC-6s operating in Canada and one is pictured here. The production models had a few changes, the most noticeable being the removal of the cover over the tag axle wheels. The MC-6 buses that were in service in the United States had the original Detroit Diesel 12V-71 engines replaced with Detroit Diesel 8V-71 engines.

and Canada bought MC-7s, including Greyhound.

The MC-6, a 102-inch-wide model introduced in 1969, was developed by MCI for Greyhound. The MC-6 and MC-7 had both been in development, but the engineering of the MC-6, which was basically an entirely new bus, required more time. As a result, the MC-7, which was adapted primarily from previous MCI models, was presented earlier. The MC-6 had a V-12 Detroit Diesel engine and was also 40 feet long. It first saw service in Canada on Greyhound routes. The 102-inch width was not legal in the United States at the time, although some states gave permission for wider intercity buses and the MC-6 was used on some routes. The bus had limited production because it turned out to be ahead of its time. MCI eventually introduced the MC-8 in 1973 and the MC-9 in 1979.

In 1986, when 102-inch-wide buses were legalized universally, MCI's 102-inch buses were designated with a model number prefixed by 102. The 102C3, introduced in the late 1980s, featured exterior panels that were fully paintable, allowing for new graphics and colorful paint schemes.

Eagle Manufacturing Co. began producing several different models during the 1980s, including the Models 10, 15 and 20. All were quite similar except that the front was modified on each new model

Motor Coach Industries introduced the Model MC-7 in 1968 and production continued until 1973. More than 2,500 MC-7 buses were built. They had a 40-foot length and three axles. Greyhound Lines in the United States purchased 1,400 units of this model. Many other companies throughout the United States and Canada added MC-7s to their fleets. This MC-7 was one of the first ones built. It had the rear tag axle wheels covered.

and 102-inch-wide bodies were introduced with the Models 15 and 20.

In the 1970s and 1980s more intercity bus companies began using vans or very small buses, often for intermodal services. Some companies continued to use stretched-out sedans, and large passenger vans were also put into service. National Coach, El Dorado, Champion and several other small manufacturers were building small buses, seating fewer than 30 passengers. At some airports, particularly Chicago's O'Hare, Boston's Logan and the San Francisco and Los Angeles airports, new bus companies began providing considerable service bringing passengers from surrounding communities into the airports. These services used both high-capacity large buses and some small buses.

In the 1990s many city bus systems throughout the nation became publicly owned. Many of these transit agencies expanded their service areas to reach out up to 30 to 50 miles for commuters. Regular transit buses were not suited for 'these extended routes and the agencies began buying intercity buses for their commuter services. There was quite an emphasis on this usage and quite a few buses sold.

Intercity buses were being used in other ways as well. Corporations were transporting workers to manufacturing sites and, particularly in California, intercity buses were being designed to transport prisoners. The U.S. Immigration Service also acquired intercity buses for transporting illegal aliens back to Mexico. Intercity bus builders found they were producing more buses without interiors for several specialty firms, such as Marathon Coach of Coburg, Oregon. These companies would design and finish the interiors as large motor homes for individuals, entertainers, business people and others. Some bus companies had special executive coaches built. These coaches had luxury seating and special refinements to appeal to VIP business people and other travelers and were offered for charter to travelers who felt they would suit their travel needs.

Greyhound Lines of Canada, Calgary, Alberta, operated 57 Motor Coach Industries MC-7 buses, one of which is pictured here. In Canada these buses were named Super 7 Scenicruisers. MC-7 models seated 47 passengers and were powered with Detroit Diesel 8V-71 diesel engines. The rear tag axle wheels were not covered, although the prototype models had covered rear wheels.

Northern Pacific Transport, a subsidiary of Northern Pacific Railway, St. Paul, Minnesota, operated buses in many areas connecting with its main line trains. Often the buses were combination truck/bus vehicles so that both passengers and freight could be carried where rail service had been abandoned. Northern Pacific Transport operated this 1962 stretched Chevrolet in Minnesota. The rail line was not abandoned but was used for freight only; therefore, the Chevrolet was used to transport passengers over the route.

Mogollon Stage Lines, Payson, Arizona, operated a small bus line that had services operating between Phoenix and Payson and Winslow, Arizona. One of the so-called buses was this 1963 Ford Econoline van. Although the bus line carried some passengers it did considerable business with packages going to a number of the small communities east of Phoenix.

A small bus company in the Blue Mountains area of Northeastern Oregon operated this 1969 Medium-Duty Dodge Crew Cab truck. Wallowa Valley Stage Line, the bus company, was obviously also a truck line at that time. The crew cab allowed it to double as a bus and carry up to six passengers.

This 1969 Pontiac Stageway stretched sedan was in service for Hudson Bus Lines, Nashua, New Hampshire. Hudson Bus Lines, which had corporate headquarters in Medford, Massachusetts, had suburban service in the Boston area and city buses in several New England cities, Nashua being one. Hudson recognized the growing need for airport service in the late 1960s, and began operating between Nashua and Boston's Logan Airport.

Sun River Stages, Great Falls, Montana, was a small bus line operating a Great Falls-Missoula, Montana route in the mid-1970s. Sun River operated two of these unusual 1973 Ford stretched vans. Clark Fork Valley Stages also operated one of these vans. Sun River Stages sold its route to Intermountain Transportation Co., Anaconda, Montana, in 1977. Rimrock Stages, Billings, Montana, now operates buses on the route.

Star Valley Jackson Stages, Idaho Falls, Idaho, connected Idaho Falls with Jackson, Wyoming in the Teton National Park area. The company operated a limited service using this 1970 Dodge van. Many small bus lines, especially in the West, found vans were very suitable for carrying a small number of passengers comfortably, along with a certain amount of baggage and packages.

Roberts Hawaii, Inc. is one of the pioneer bus companies on the Hawaiian Islands. Roberts had its start in 1944 on the island of Kauai and later expanded to other islands. In 1964 Roberts Ilima Tours and Sightseeing was established. One of its first large buses was this high-level bus built by Crown Coach Corporation in 1967. Roberts expanded and became the largest sightseeing and tour operator in Hawaii.

Crown Coach Corporation, Los Angeles, California, mainly a builder of school buses, also built some commercial buses of various types. Cargo coaches were among some of the special vehicles produced by Crown. This 1968 model was a combination truck/bus built for Great Northern Transport Company, a subsidiary of the Great Northern Railway Company. It is pictured here at Plentywood, Montana.

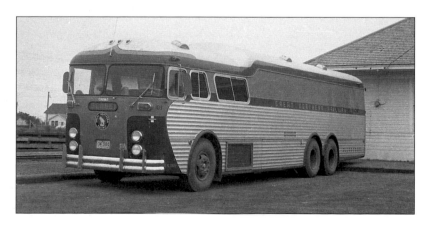

Carpenter Body Works, Inc., Mitchell, Indiana, an important builder of school buses, produced some buses for intercity service. This Model CS340 6 was made available in 1969. It featured a Cummins diesel engine mounted in the rear. Although the Carpenter company began prior to 1923, that was the year when it first began building school buses.

Zephyr Lines, Minneapolis, Minnesota, purchased this GM Model PD 4107 bus in 1966. The Model PD 4107 was a popular bus for smaller companies as well as for larger ones. There was a step-up seating arrangement in the front and an upper level windshield. The original Zephyr Lines began in 1937, operating a line between Minneapolis and Ashland, Wisconsin. Zephyr Lines was purchased by Liederbach Bus Co., a pioneer Minnesota bus company, in 1953.

The General Motors Model PD 4107 was produced between 1966 and 1969 and 1,267 were built. It was a 35-foot bus, powered by a Detroit Diesel 8V-71 engine. Peerless Stages, Oakland, California, received one of the first GM PD 4107 buses in 1966. Two more were added the following year and some secondhand PD 4107 buses joined the fleet later. Peerless Stages has the distinction of being one of the oldest bus lines in the country. It began in 1918 and served several routes in the East Bay area.

Grey Goose Bus Line, Winnipeg, Manitoba, had expanded after World War II and was serving many remote communities in Northern Manitoba. Some of the highways used by Grey Goose buses were not hard surfaced for distances of 160 miles or more. This 1976 GM P8M 4108 was one used in Northern Manitoba. It was originally owned by the Grey Goose company known as Yellow Coach of Edmonton, Alberta. The GM buses at the time were best suited to the conditions of the roads in the north. Note the dust on the highways as the two buses pass, and the air scoop high on the rear corner of the bus.

CHAPTER 9

Larger Buses

Charter and tour services became more important in the 1960s as the population became more mobile. Travel was becoming a very competitive business, with marketing becoming a necessity. Because some thought the word "bus" was not appropriate for the new, modern services, the words "motorcoach" and "coach" began to be used more frequently.

Before the civil-rights movement of the 1960s intercity bus services in the South, just as in the city bus industry, had been segregated for many years. Seating for African-Americans was restricted to the back of the bus, and there were separate restrooms and restaurants for black and white patrons in bus terminals. When Rosa Parks refused to give up her seat on a city bus in Montgomery, Alabama in 1955, her courageous stand started the movement which would eventually end segregation on both city and intercity buses.

In 1971 the U.S. government began operating Amtrak long-distance passenger rail service. The privately funded intercity bus industry was opposed to the new service, seeing it as unfair competition

Wisconsin-Michigan Coaches, Green Bay, Wisconsin, bought this GM PD 4903 bus in 1968, the year the model was introduced. It was a 40-foot bus and had an option of retractable extra wheels or a three-axle configuration. Wisconsin-Michigan Coaches began in 1968. Wisconsin-Michigan joined the National Trailways Bus System in 1987, and two years later the company ceased operations.

In 1968, GM Truck & Coach Division introduced the Model PD 4903 40-foot bus. It had a step-up front seating, although most of the 37 seats were on a higher level. This bus was available as a two-axle version, which was popular in the Northeast United States where 40-foot buses could operate legally with two axles. A third retractable set of wheels ahead of the driving axle was available to operators requiring three-axle buses.

from the publicly supported rail service. Over time, however, Amtrak presented new opportunities for some bus companies that were able to provide bus service for discontinued rail routes as well as connecting service with Amtrak from cities that weren't on Amtrak routes. However, competition with Amtrak trains still remained on long-distance services and on some routes, and Amtrak was still basically opposed by the private intercity industry.

In 1973 and 1974 oil-producing nations cut off supplies of oil to the United States and other large importers. Although obtaining fuel during the oil crisis wasn't necessarily a problem for the bus industry, diesel prices rose dramatically. Some intercity bus companies resorted to adding a surcharge on bus tickets. The fuel crisis caused a temporary boost in travelers for the intercity bus industry, but after the crisis abated bus travel began to decline.

Although oil shipments eventually increased, the world's way of thinking was changed forever. Dependence on fossil fuel became an important concern. Lower speed limits were imposed on all highway traffic, and new vehicle designs were introduced, intended to reduce weight and wind resistance. Research began on alternative fuels and new engines such as turbines. However, turbine power didn't provide a direction for new engine technology, and although natural gas engines were being used for city bus fleets, natural gas engines were not appropriate for intercity buses.

The Deregulation Act of 1982 was responsible for much of the significant change that took place thereafter in the U.S. bus industry. Deregulation meant that bus companies could set their own fares. Also, anyone could operate routes that were formerly protected from competition. However, anyone operating interstate buses was required to have adequate insurance and comply with strict safety standards. Most states continued to have some controls and regulations for buses operating within a state.

Deregulation, along with the growing dominance of the automobile, caused the discontinuance of some intercity bus service. Many cities, even some with populations of 25,000 to 30,000, found themselves without intercity bus service. Some states began subsidizing intercity bus companies for routes that had been discontinued and a certain amount of intercity service was duly provided by regional or state public agencies.

In addition to the loss of service to many cities, intercity bus companies also found themselves losing revenues to package express companies. However, the bus companies seemed to have captured a certain amount of package express service because they provided that service every day of the week as well as evenings. They were able to retain their niche in that respect, but they still couldn't compete with other courier services. However, despite the competition from other couriers, Canadian carriers continued to do a considerable amount of package express business. Some operators began carrying trailers behind their buses for their package business, and even used trucks on some routes. Greyhound of Canada continued to emphasize carrying packages and freight to remote Canadian communities.

Touring services became increasingly important in the late 1980s and '90s. The travel industry had a number of tour companies that were able to charter buses from regular bus companies, and that partnership proved to be very successful. Bus manufacturers continued to design buses to cater to the tour passenger. The installation of airline-style luggage racks and the addition of carpet on the sides, floors and even the ceiling made the interiors look very attractive. By the 1980s almost all intercity buses had lavatories in the rear.

In 1990, the ADA (Americans with Disabilities Act) brought about a need for intercity bus companies to provide handicapped accessible buses. This allowed some companies to start a new type of business because they were never able to accommodate the handicapped population in the past. It was also important because the population in general was aging and the elderly welcomed the opportunity to continue traveling, even though they weren't otherwise ambulatory.

Other government regulations also affected the bus industry. The Commercial Drivers License Law was passed early in the decade to allow for nationwide background checks on drivers and driver candidates. The Motor Carrier Safety Act emphasized stricter rules for commercial drivers and new motor carriers. Safety had always been important to the bus industry and its record had been outstanding. However, these new rules put even more emphasis

Richfield Bus Company, Bloomington, Minnesota, began as a suburban transit line in the Minneapolis area in 1959. The company expanded and later emphasized their charter services. In 1968 this GM Model 4903 was purchased for the charter business. The PD 4903 was a 40-foot bus that was proving to be popular with both large and small bus companies as charter business was becoming competitive and there was a trend toward attractive luxury buses.

Western New York Motor Lines, Inc., Batavia, New York, bought this GM PD 4905 in 1970, the year the model, which replaced the Model PD 4903, was introduced. The changes were insignificant and the optional set of rear wheels and the Detroit Diesel 9V-71 engine continued. Western New York Motor Lines began in 1924. Following World War II Western joined the National Trailways Bus System and chose the name Empire Trailways. In 1994 the company was acquired by Adirondack Trailways, Kingston, New York, and became New York Trailways.

Motor Coach Industries (MCI) introduced the Model MC-8 in 1973. It had a number of changes from the Model MC-7 of 1968. The windshield was enlarged and instead of having the destination sign above the windshield, it was placed in a box inside at the top of the right side windshield. The MC-8 had a flat floor with a slightly inclined aisle ramp. Greyhound Lines purchased a total of 2,550 units of the MC-8 buses.

on safe driving and safer buses. As a result the bus industry received many safety awards and favorable publicity for its safety efforts.

In addition, the federal government ruled that CFC-based (chlorofluorocarbon-based) refrigerants would have to be phased out and new, ozone-friendly refrigerants had to be used.

One of the most important innovations of the 1980s was the introduction of electronic controls for diesel engines. Detroit Diesel Allison announced Detroit Diesel Electronic Controls (DDEC) for its diesel engines in 1985. The company also introduced a new four-cycle, heavy-duty diesel engine, the Series 60, for the bus market. Cummins Engine Company began offering its L-10 four-cycle, turbocharged diesel engine to the bus industry in 1985. In 1995, Cummins offered a new four-cycle diesel engine, the M-11E, for large buses. It succeeded the successful L-10. Cummins engines were also very popular for small buses. The new engines, as well as electronic controls, brought about better economy and performance for the buses.

There was interest in automatic transmissions for intercity buses. Allison Transmission introduced its World Transmission in 1992. Although the Al-

Blue Bird Coach Lines, Olean, New York, grew from a small taxi company in 1919 to an important tour and charter operation in a number of cities. The company also operated some intercity service. Blue Bird aggressively promoted its services and expanded, first to Buffalo and then to other cities. One of Blue Bird's Motor Coach Industries MC-8 buses was attractively painted to celebrate the Bicentennial of the United States in 1976. Blue Bird operated 25 MC-8 buses, acquiring its first six in 1974.

In 1980, four Motor Coach Industries (MCI) Model MC-8 Greyhound Lines buses were involved in a demonstration of turbine engines. The program was sponsored by the U.S. Department of Energy. Earlier bus turbine engines were tested with Greyhound MC-7 buses. The turbine buses operated for a time in revenue service between Chicago and Cincinnati. Lack of funding brought the program to a close after a short time and it was never renewed.

Yellowstone Park Company, Mammoth Hot Springs, Wyoming, was the concessionaire to provide transportation for visitors in Yellowstone National Park in 1975. At that time and the following year, 25 Motor Coach Industries MC-5B buses were acquired for this service. The Model MC-5B buses were first built in 1971 and manufacturing continued until 1977. They changed little from the MC-5A model. These Model MC-5B buses saw many years of service in Yellowstone National Park.

lison Transmission came into use first and was the primary automatic transmission in use on buses in the United States, two German manufacturers, ZF Industries and Voith Transmissions, also entered the North American market with automatic transmissions for buses. Eaton Industries, a U.S. manufacturer, also offered a semiautomatic transmission, but it wasn't chosen by a majority of the bus owners.

Multiplex and similar improved wiring systems became available in 1995. Improved tires, air conditioning, paint, brakes and other components were also introduced in the 1990s.

Paint schemes became wilder, with more graphics. Sometimes scenic tourism spots or historic scenes were portrayed on the buses to create more interest in tours. Some companies, particularly Greyhound, used wraparound advertising designs but they didn't prove to be overly popular because the designs over the windows restricted the view of the passengers.

In the late 1990s a move began which resulted in the consolidation of a number of bus companies. While this concept seemed new and was unheard-of by much of the industry, consolidation was really nothing new. It actually began with Greyhound and others in the early 1930s and continued in later years. The newest round of consolidations in the 1990s resulted in the formation of a company called Coach USA (which was known in Canada as Coach Canada) and later was acquired by the British company Stagecoach Group. Global Passenger Services (GPS) also began a consolidation program about the same time, as did Greyhound.

Motor Coach Industries (MCI) had begun building and selling the Model MC-5 in the United States in 1964. The MC-5 was a 35-foot bus and was followed by the MC-5B, which featured minor changes. In 1977, when the MC-5C was introduced, there were several noticeable changes, including a new front and other design changes. Production of the MC-5C ended in 1980. It was the last 35-foot bus built by MCI until the 1990s. One of the companies operating an MC-5C bus, which is pictured, was Orleans Transportation Co., New Orleans, Louisiana, the Gray Line operator in the area.

Red Top Sedan Service, Miami, Florida, was a subsidiary of the Greyhound Corporation. It served passengers arriving at the Miami International Airport. In 1971, this Setra low-profile bus was introduced into the service. The Setra was a product of Karl Kassbohrer, AG, of Stuttgart, Germany. Red Top Sedan Service was also involved with the American Sightseeing Service in the area at the time.

National Custom Van Corporation of Yonkers, and later Mt. Vernon, New York, introduced four models of a bus especially designed for airport services in 1979. The bus models were built from Ford E350 vans. The vans were lengthened for 13 to 19-passenger capacities with an aisle and one-and-two seating arrangements. The vans were also heightened. This National Custom Van was in airport service for Connecticut Limousine Service, Milford, Connecticut.

Many small bus lines in the 1980s saw their passenger numbers diminishing and turned to using vans. One of these companies was Bickel Bus Line of Norton, Kansas. It served a 110-mile, north-south route in Western Kansas between Norton and Dodge City. Pictured is a 1984 15-passenger van, the "Flagship" of the Bickel Bus Line company. When this picture was taken in 1988 Bickel Bus Line was celebrating its 60th anniversary.

Bus service to remote parts of Canada's Yukon Territory was not possible until suitable roads were built. North West Stages began service with Ford vans in 1988. The service ran between the company's base in Whitehorse, Yukon to Ross River and Faro, Yukon thrice weekly, a distance of more than 200 miles (350 kilometers) each way. This service was typical of a number of similar services in the far north.

Continental Air Transport Company, Chicago, Illinois, operated large buses for many years to transport airline passengers from Chicago's O'Hare and Midway Airports to downtown Chicago and its suburban areas. In 1985 Continental found that operating large buses was too costly and inefficient for airport services. It was a challenge to make a change, but Continental Air Transport made the successful move to vans. One of the 1988 Continental Dodge vans is pictured here.

In 1991, on the 75th anniversary of Red Ball Stage Line of Klamath Falls, Oregon, this 1986 Ford van was making the daily round trip between Klamath Falls and Lakeview, Oregon, a distance of 96 miles. Red Ball Stage Line is one of the numerous small bus lines that surmounted many challenges in the bus business and continued to serve an important need to a rural population.

The Motor Coach Industries Model MC-9 was one of America's most popular intercity buses. It was launched in 1979 and continued in production into the early 1990s. The MC-9 had changes from the MC-8; in particular, a roofline that was at the same level from front to back and large side windows. Greyhound Lines had the largest fleet of MC-9 buses, with a total of 1,950. Transportation Manufacturing Co., Roswell, New Mexico, which was a part of Motor Coach Industries, built the Greyhound MC-9 buses.

In the 1980s bus companies were placing an emphasis on tours. Carl R. Bieber, Inc., Kutztown, Pennsylvania, was one of the companies that was very active in tours and was commonly known as Bieber Tourways. Tours to the casinos in Atlantic City, New Jersey were popular and Bieber buses were colorfully painted with the names of casinos to attract customers. Bieber was one of the first bus companies to acquire Motor Coach Industries MC-9 buses, with the first four added in 1979.

Although the Motor Coach Industries Model MC-9 remained unchanged for the nearly 15 years the bus was in production, there were some changes from the original as a result of specification options by some operators. This MC-9 of Gray Coach Lines, Toronto, Ontario, reflects one of the changes, with the noticeable two-leaf door. The two-leaf door was popular for companies like Gray Coach for commuter service.

In 1984 Gray Line of Alaska used one of its Motor Coach Industries MC-9 buses to commemorate the 25th anniversary of Alaskan statehood. Beginning in the 1980s various bus companies began using one or more of their buses for advertising the areas served or services offered. Gray Line of Alaska had its start in 1947 as Westours Motorcoaches, Inc. *Mark Gregg*

The Anderson House, Wabasha, Minnesota, has been unique in many ways. The hotel, which was built in 1858, was refurbished in the mid-1970s. It became a celebrated tourist attraction with many tour customers. Seeing all the tour buses stopping at the hotel, John Hall of the Anderson House began the Anderson House tour division and operated tours nationwide. This Motor Coach Industries MC-9 bus, parked in front of the historic hotel, was one of the buses used on tours in 1987. The Anderson House story is not complete without telling about the in-house cats. If one stays at the Anderson House overnight a cat can be requested as a bed-warming companion.

New Jersey Transit (NJ Transit), Maplewood, New Jersey, acquired 1,115 Motor Coach Industries MC-9 buses in the mid-1980s. These buses were primarily the standard MC-9 models, but NJ Transit specified that the destination sign, with a large opening, be mounted above the windshield. NJ Transit, a public agency, operated a number of intercity buses throughout New Jersey. The MC-9 pictured here is a 1987 model.

In the 1980s bus companies were carrying a considerable amount of package express. In order to accommodate increased volume on some routes, Trailways, Inc. converted some of its Model 01 Eagle buses into combination vehicles. The rear section of the buses was made into a package-carrying section and the front continued to accommodate passengers. This Eagle Model 01 was originally built in the 1960s.

Motor Coach Industries (MCI), Winnipeg, Manitoba, introduced new models in 1984. They were the 96A3 and the 96A2. The following year the 102A3 and the 102A2 models were announced. The 96 and the 102 refer to the width in inches and the 2 and 3 refer to the number of axles. Although there were a number of changes from the previous Model MC-9, which continued in production, the most noticeable change was the front, with a slanting windshield streamlining the frontal appearance. DeNure Tours, Chatham, Ontario, acquired four MCI Model 102A3 buses in 1986. DeNure Tours was a part of Chatham Coach Lines.

Prevost Car, Inc. introduced the Marathon XL in 1983. It was the first 102-inch-wide bus produced by Prevost. The design was similar to the Le Mirage model but had standard-sized windows on the sides which did not extend into the roof like the windows on the Le Mirage models. The Marathon was particularly designed for intercity services, but it never sold in great numbers.

International Influence

In the 1980s European influences began to impact new bus designs in the United States. Many Americans traveling in Europe experienced the ultra-luxurious buses found there. In addition, many Europeans and other foreign visitors were coming to the U.S. and demanding a more luxurious bus for their tours and charters than the usual day-to-day intercity bus. U.S. manufacturers had to respond to these influences, and they did.

Bus manufacturers and bus companies continued to refine the interiors of their buses, with better lighting, bigger windows and other changes to attract the more demanding clientele. Seats were considerably improved and now included footrests. In some cases seats were designed so that they could be turned around to face each other, often with a table between them. There were also fold-down tables in the seats. A significant change was the introduction of video entertainment systems. With videos, passengers could be entertained while they

The Mercedes-Benz Model 0-302-40, built in Germany, was introduced in the United States in 1968. A number of sightseeing companies bought the new European-style bus. Rawding Lines, the Gray Line Sightseeing franchisee in Boston, Massachusetts, was one of these companies. The Model 0-302-40, which was very popular in Europe and elsewhere, had a Mercedes-Benz 0M355 diesel engine.

A Belgian luxury bus manufacturer PVBA LAG SPRL of Bree, Belgium began marketing buses in the United States with a subsidiary, LAG Motorcoaches, Bel Air, Maryland. Two models were presented beginning in 1984. The most popular was the LAG 350 T, a 40-foot, three-axle bus equipped with a Cummins L-10 diesel engine. Sunnyland Stages, Springfield, Missouri, acquired this LAG 350 T in 1987. Sunnyland Stages began in 1936 with a Springfield-Harrison, Arkansas intercity route. The company began emphasizing charters and tours, and route services ended in 1984.

were traveling and could also watch videos of coming attractions they would be visiting.

Prevost Car, Inc. of Canada entered the U.S. market in 1968. In 1973 Prevost introduced its Prestige model, which featured large passenger windows extending slightly into the roofline, a very popular feature with the growing charter/tour market. The company's popular Le Mirage model, introduced in 1976, was similar to the Prestige, but the step-up front was changed to a full front and it featured a four-part windshield. With its H3-40 model, introduced in 1980, Prevost offered new styling and many innovations. Deliveries of Prevost's revolutionary H5-60 articulated intercity coach began in the 1980s. The H5-60 had five axles and was 60 feet long, but it had limited popularity. In 1992, soon after 45-foot buses were legalized, the

company introduced the H3-45, and the H3-40 became the H3-41.

Mercedes-Benz introduced its O302 model to the United States as early as 1968. It was one of the first modern introductions of a European coach in the United States. However, the first European-based bus manufacturer to begin building European-style buses in the United States was the German manufacturer Neoplan. The company built a plant in Lamar, Colorado in 1981. Operating as Neoplan USA Corporation, the company built charter and tour coaches as well as transit buses.

Kassbohrer of Ulm, Germany, which built Eagle buses for Trailways in the 1950s, entered the U.S. market in 1984, selling intercity buses under the Setra name. Setra added a 45-foot bus to its U.S. market line in 1995 and continued featuring its European-styled model, which had been introduced in the 1980s. Setra is now a part of the DaimlerChrysler organization.

Van Hool NV of Belgium entered the intercity coach market in the early 1980s. Its buses were built in Europe and shipped to the United States. At first

The Gottlob Auwarter KG firm was one of several bus builders in Germany. Its buses were known by the name Neoplan. In 1981 the company saw opportunities in establishing a presence in the United States. A Neoplan bus building facility was opened in Lamar, Colorado at that time. A variety of intercity and transit buses were built, including double-deck N122/3 Skyliner models. Lorenz Bus Service, Minneapolis, Minnesota, operated this Skyliner bus and two others in charter service.

The German bus and truck manufacturer Maschinen-fabrik Augsburg Nurenberg AG (MAN) began selling city buses in the United States. A MAN Truck & Bus Corporation was established with a plant to build the buses in 1980. Some MAN Model SR tour and charter buses were sold by VIP Tours, Orlando, Florida, at the same time. The buses were bought secondhand from European operators, then refurbished and marketed in the United States. Pictured here is one of the 1986 MAN SR buses operated by Emerald Empire Charter Service, Inc. of Eugene, Oregon. By the late 1980s this program for MAN tour and charter buses ended.

Mack Trucks, Allentown, Pennsylvania, tried to re-enter the bus business in 1985, when it introduced the Model FR-1 bus with great fanfare at an industry event. The new bus was built in France by Renault, which had a majority ownership in Mack Trucks. It was a two-axle, 40-foot bus and had a Mack EG 335 diesel engine. It did not sell, mainly because it didn't meet all the requirements of the intercity bus industry in the United States.

a limited number of buses were sold. Then, in 1987, ABC Bus of Faribault, Minnesota was appointed exclusive U.S. distributor of Van Hool coaches. The partnership proved very successful and sales of Van Hool buses grew dramatically. At first a 40-foot model was marketed, known as the T-815. Then Van Hool presented its 45-foot bus, the T800-45, to the U.S. market in 1993. The T-2140 and T-2145 models followed.

Motor Coach Industries (MCI) introduced a number of new models. In 1991 the smooth-sided B models were unveiled. Soon after, the C model, also with smooth, paintable sides and a higher body, was introduced. The D models came in 1992 in both 40- and 45-foot versions. Also that year the MC-12, modified from the successful MC-9 model, went into production for Greyhound Lines. The MC-12 offered important economies following difficult years for Greyhound.

MCI introduced the E model, known as the Renaissance, in 1996. It was designed mainly for tour service and featured a new, modern style and

Mack Trucks first introduced the French-built Renault FR-1 bus in 1985, but bus companies did not place the orders that were expected. The bus had two axles and a 40-foot length, which was not legally accepted on the highways in most areas. Therefore, Mack introduced this three-axle Model FR-1 bus in 1989. Like the original FR-1, it did not find interest among bus operators and the Mack intercity bus venture of the 1980s ended in 1989.

Neoplan USA, Lamar, Colorado, began building the AN340 bus in 1984. It was called the Metroliner and was designed mainly as a commuter bus for transit agencies. It was available as a two- or three-axle bus and the standard engine was the Detroit Diesel 8V-92. The County of Hawaii Transit Agency, Hilo, Hawaii, purchased seven Metroliner buses in 1994 for service around the island between Hilo and Kona.

numerous new features, including a curved entrance stairway. The G model, particularly designed for use by Greyhound, was presented late in 1999. Greyhound Lines began operating G model buses soon afterward. A J model, much like the E model, was offered and was seen as more practical for long-distance intercity service.

Blue Bird Body Corporation, in Fort Valley, Georgia, a major builder of school buses and transit buses, had also been building luxury motor home buses. In 1997, using the same basic body, the company introduced a 40-foot intercity model known as the LTC-40.

The Dina Viaggio model bus was introduced in 1994. It was assembled in Mexico with a Brazilian Marcopolo body by Consorcio G Grupo Dina SA de CV, which at that time owned Motor Coach Industries. The Dina Viaggio was marketed with Motor Coach Industries buses in the U.S. and Canada.

The culture of the United States bus industry is very different from that in other countries. Resistance to change, long-term family ownership, the widespread use of the automobile, and the long distances involved in bus operations have often influenced it. In a number of cases foreign organizations in both the operations and manufacturing sectors, which had entered into the ownership and management of bus operations in the United States, found it difficult to adapt to the unique bus industry culture. Some overseas investors who were unable to adapt found it necessary to downsize or discontinue their investment in U.S. bus operations.

In 1968, the 05 model Eagle was introduced. It was similar to the Model 01, but had a newly styled front and the driving axle was moved to the rear of the tandem arrangement. Bus and Car NV in Belgium first built it in 1968. In 1974 the Eagle International, Inc. company was formed, and a new factory was established in Brownsville, Texas to build Eagle buses. Wilson Bus Lines, East Templeton, Massachusetts, owned this Eagle 05 bus.

The Model 10S Eagle bus was introduced in 1982. It had two, instead of three, axles on a 40-foot body length. It was a bus designed for public transportation authorities, which at that time were interested in purchasing more luxury buses for longer commuter services. At the time, New Trails, Inc., a holding company, owned the Eagle company. The new Model 10S was manufactured at a new plant in Harlingen, Texas. The Model 10S and 10LT did not produce many customers and the plant in Harlingen closed soon after it was opened.

Eagle International, Brownsville, Texas, introduced the Model 10 Eagle bus in 1980. Its front appearance was changed from previous models. There were full side windows and the top opening sections found on the Model 05 Eagle buses were eliminated. Zanetti Bus Line of Rock Springs, Wyoming was the owner of this Eagle Model 10 bus in 1985. Zanetti Bus Line began in 1967 with an intercity line in Southwestern Wyoming. The company also did considerable contract work for coal mining companies in the area.

Johnson Bus, Inc., Elizabethtown, Pennsylvania, bought two Model 15 Eagle buses in 1986. The Model 15 was the first Eagle bus to be built with a 102-inch body. The front of this model had a large one-piece window. A Detroit Diesel 6V-92TA engine was standard. Johnson Bus, Inc. began in 1938 as a school bus operation and in 1955 began operating charters and tours. Can-Am Tours is part of the company.

Eagle International, Inc., first presented the Eagle Model 15/35 35-foot, two-axle bus in 1988 in Brownsville, Texas. It was thought that a 35-foot bus would have some appeal to operators of charter and tour services, as well as for commuter and airport operations. This model did not attract too many customers, although some were sold as luxury motor homes. At the time Greyhound Lines owned Eagle International.

In 1988 Eagle Bus Manufacturing Co., Brownsville, Texas, won a bid to supply New Jersey Transit, Morristown, New Jersey, with 119 Eagle Model 20 buses. These buses were not the typical Eagle buses in appearance. New Jersey Transit required a different front, designed with a large destination sign opening. These buses were 96 inches wide and had stainless steel on the lower sides. A Detroit Diesel 6V-92TA diesel engine powered the buses. They did not prove to be overly satisfactory and were withdrawn from service a few years later.

This Model 20 45-foot Eagle bus and ten others were ordered in late 1989 by Saskatchewan Transportation Company, Regina, Saskatchewan. At the time, Eagle Bus Manufacturing Co. had come under the control of Greyhound Lines following Greyhound's acquisition of Trailways, Inc. These buses were involved in some controversial circumstances with the purchase. In addition, they did not prove satisfactory to Saskatchewan Transportation Co. and by 1995 they were no longer in the fleet.

Bonanza Bus Lines, Providence, Rhode Island, acquired ten Model 96A2 buses in 1986 from Transportation Manufacturing Company, Roswell, New Mexico, a subsidiary of Motor Coach Industries (MCI). The Model 96A2 was a two-axle bus that was made available to companies in the East, which could legally operate 40-foot buses with two axles. The A series MCI buses were made available beginning in 1985. Bonanza Bus Lines began in 1930 and operated a main route between Providence, Rhode Island and New York and also routes into Boston and Cape Cod.

The Prevost Model H5-60 articulated bus was announced in 1985. It had five axles and was 60 feet long. It had a Detroit Diesel 8V-92TTA diesel engine mounted in the front unit under the floor. Styling of the new bus was very modern with a large four-piece high windshield and large side windows. A number of bus companies purchased this model for charter and tour service. In Canada, Orleans Express had H5-60 buses on regular route services.

The Alaska Yukon Explorer Lounge Coaches went into service in 1991. At that time 14 Prevost Model H5-60 articulated buses were chosen by Holland America Lines-Westours, Seattle, Washington, for this special service. After considerable testing in cold weather and on highways subject to permafrost, the Prevost articulated buses went into service and brought a new era of travel to tour customers in the Alaska-Yukon market. The H5-60 buses had special two-and-one seating for 52 passengers and a special lounge in the rear cabin.

The first Van Hool of Belgium bus that was introduced into the United States in 1986 was the Acron T-815 model. This model had a seating capacity of 49 passengers and had an optional second door. A MAN diesel engine powered the T-815 model. Scenic Stage Line, Morrison, Illinois, took delivery of this Acron T-815 bus in 1988. Scenic Stage Line, a company involved in charter and school bus service, later acquired three similar Van Hool buses. Scenic Stage Line began in 1942.

Van Hool, the Belgian bus manufacturer, built a small Model T-809 Alizee bus, which was sold by the U.S. distributor, ABC Companies of Faribault, Minnesota beginning in 1987. It was a 30- to 37-passenger bus with a length of 28.3 feet. This type of bus was suited for airport shuttles and for some charter and tour work. A MAN under-floor engine was standard. North Atlanta Coach & Transportation, also known as Northside Airport Express, Atlanta, Georgia, which operated this bus, had its start in 1974.

Buses built by Karl Kassbohrer, AG, Stuttgart, Germany, were not new to the United States in 1984 when Setra buses of that company were introduced. Previously, the Kassbohrer company had built Eagle buses for Trailways companies. The Setra bus model sold in the United States was the Model S215HDH, named the Intercontinental. Mechanically the Setra buses had American components. Greenlawn Transit Lines of Columbus, Ohio purchased the Setra bus pictured here in 1991. This company, which began in 1953, is also known as Bus One.

In the early days of bus transportation bus bodies were built on truck chassis. This procedure returned in the 1980s. A number of manufacturers began building bodies on what have been called cutaway truck chassis. Champion Motor Coach, Inc., Imlay City, Michigan, became a large producer of this type of bus. Shown here is a Champion bus of 1991 in service by the Alaska Intercity Bus Line, which operated between Homer and Anchorage, Alaska.

In 1996, at the time of Saskatchewan Transportation Company's 50th anniversary, the Regina-based company began operating small buses in order to continue to serve routes with fewer passengers. Pictured here is one of the 21-passenger Goshen-bodied Ford buses that entered service. Four 35-passenger ElDorado mid-sized buses were also added to the fleet.

In 1990 the Argentine firm commonly known as Cametal presented a bus with a very different design to the United States market. It was known as the CX-40. The sharp, aerodynamic front tapered upward from the front bumper to the roofline. In 1990-1991, Mears Transportation Group, Orlando, Florida, bought eight of these unusual buses, one of which is pictured here. The CX-40s were 40-foot models. A 32-foot Cametal was also built and Mears owned four of them.

Thomas Built Buses, High Point, North Carolina, offered this bus for tour and charter services in the early 1990s. It was called the Chartour and was available in several lengths, with seating for between 37 and 45 passengers, depending on the length of the bus. Rear-mounted Caterpillar or Cummins engines were available. The Thomas name has a long history in transportation, beginning as the Perley A. Thomas Car Works building streetcars, then trolley buses and school buses. School buses have been an important part of the Thomas company. By the 1960s commercial buses were being produced in the Thomas factories.

Hino Autobody, Ltd., Tokyo, Japan, is one of the largest producers of buses in the world. But almost no Hino buses are in service in the United States or Canada. An exception is Hawaii. This Hino bus along with 16 others is in the Travel Plaza Transportation fleet in Honolulu. Hino buses were first produced after World War II.

Buses of Today and the Future

Bus manufacturers are always looking forward to innovations in the design of buses as well as in technology. No doubt the industry will see further improvements and new ideas incorporated into its buses, not only for safety, reliability and performance, but also for the comfort and convenience of the passengers.

Tour operators have expanded their operations by packaging trips to sporting events, shopping excursions, casino trips, holiday attractions, and even live television performances. Those companies that make their products attractive by combining interesting destinations with safe and comfortable vehicles will be certain to have success. New, innovative marketing tools will be introduced to encourage more people to find bus travel attractive.

Because national parks have become saturated with automobile traffic, bus service is being utilized in parks more and more. Plans are being made for more bus services to relieve the congestion.

In 2001 Motor Coach Industries (MCI) introduced the Model J4500 bus and Peter Pan Bus Lines, Springfield, Massachusetts, placed an order for 12 of these buses soon afterward. Peter Pan Bus Lines, which began in 1933, initially served a Springfield-Boston corridor. A major route expansion came in 1986 when service to New York City was added. Then, in 1992, a Washington, Baltimore and Philadelphia service began. Peter Pan has been an MCI customer since 1974. Prior to ordering the J models the company had a fleet of almost 100 D4500 model MCI buses.

Long-distance bus operators are finding passengers using their services for even longer trips than in previous years, with travelers often going two or three days on the same bus. On intercity bus services, stops are made at truck stops and convenience stores to make trips more comfortable and pleasant.

More intercity bus companies are equipping their buses with accessible lifts in answer to the demands of handicapped travelers and the requirements of the government to address accessibility issues.

Long-distance bus providers are more conscious of making trips intermodal and are offering more airport service. Rather than long-distance buses serving all communities, they are finding that rural service can now offer satisfactory connections for the public. Bus terminals are frequently intermodal terminals, often municipally or regionally owned.

Bus companies have had to increase security as a result of the terrorist attacks on September 11, 2001. In some places random checks of passengers are performed. However, because of the extended times for security at airports, in some cases bus companies have been able to offer services that can compete with the airlines. With the use of freeways and highway speeds, trips of less than 200 miles on the bus can be comparable with airline travel time.

Oregon Coachways, Inc., Eugene, Oregon, acquired this Prevost Le Mirage 45-foot bus in 1998, adding to its fleet of other Prevost Le Mirage buses. Oregon Coachways is a charter, tour and contract bus company, which began in 1983. One of its operations is a thruway service as a connection for Amtrak trains. The 45-foot Prevost Le Mirage was first made available in 1995 after being offered initially as motor homes and entertainer coaches.

Rimrock Stages, Billings, Montana, which started on a small scale in Montana in 1972, expanded and eventually assumed most of the service of Intermountain Transportation Company, which ceased business in 1995. In 2001 Rimrock bought this Prevost Model H3-41 bus. When 45-foot buses became legalized and Prevost introduced the H3-45 bus, the H3-41 bus replaced the H3-40 model to offer improved seating space.

Mid-American Coaches, Washington, Missouri, took delivery of two Prevost H3-41 buses, one of which is pictured here in 1996. These buses had a new deep red and green color scheme. Mid-American, which began in 1927, was originally known as Washington-Union-St. Louis Bus Co., and served the cities in its name. Charter and tour service became their primary business and eventually the name was changed. The Prevost H3-41 model was introduced in 1994, replacing the H3-40 model.

Intercity, charter and tour bus companies have obtained funding from the federal government for enhanced security for their services; however, efforts continue to increase that funding. In addition, bus companies will be offering more protection for drivers, who in the past have been subject to attacks.

Communication has improved on buses. Long-distance carriers are equipping their drivers with cell phones and other improved communication devices. The use of Global Positioning Systems (GPS) can enhance the safety and help improve long-distance, and even rural and short-line, bus services, as well as charter and tour operations. The future will probably bring more electronic innovations to the bus industry. It is certain the bus industry will be watching for these and other improvements.

Clean air continues to be an important topic. Engine manufacturers will continue to upgrade electronic systems to control emissions and the new "clean diesels" will be in demand. Alternative fuels and improved engines will continue to receive attention. Fuel cells and battery-electric power show promise for the future. New propulsion systems will be introduced along with new and exciting electronics to help reduce emissions, enhance safety, improve efficiency and increase comfort. Maintenance procedures will be improved, as well as programs for dispatching, planning and marketing.

United Limo, Osceola, Indiana, was operating an airport connecting service between Milwaukee and Chicago's O'Hare Airport in the 1990s. In 1991, ten Van Hool Model T-800 buses went into service. In 1995 United Limo acquired ten more Model T-800 buses, one of which is pictured here. United Limo began in 1979 and is one of the many bus companies that serve airports throughout the United States and Canada.

Yankee Line, South Boston, Massachusetts, acquired four Van Hool Model T-800-45 buses in 1996, one of which is pictured here. The company, which began in 1980, operates charters and tours, and a short commuter route. Many tour and charter operators have chosen the 45-foot Van Hool T-800-45 bus. The U.S. distributor, ABC Companies of Faribault, Minnesota, introduced this model late in 1992. Some changes from previous models were made. The Cummins L10-330E was the standard engine.

Mears Transportation Group, Orlando, Florida, has been an important tour, charter and contract operator in Central Florida since 1987. One of its contracts is with the Disney Cruise Line. In 1997, 45 Van Hool Model T2145 buses were purchased to operate this service. These buses featured a special nostalgia paint design as shown here. The Van Hool Model T2145 bus was introduced in 1997. It is a 45-foot model and is offered with either a Cummins or Detroit Diesel engine.

Princess Tours, Seattle, Washington, purchased this Van Hool Model T2145 with four others in 1999 through the national distributor, ABC Companies, Faribault, Minnesota. These buses are lift equipped and have Cummins M-11 diesel engines. Princess Tours began in 1985 as Royal Highway Tours, providing support to its cruise ship program in Alaska.

ABC Companies delivered the first two Van Hool C2045L buses to Greyhound Lines, Inc., carrying the Greyhound name and logo, on March 9, 2002. After a test of approximately 40 Van Hool C2045 buses with Greyhound's subsidiary companies in line haul and charter service for almost two years, Greyhound accepted two units for test in the Greyhound fleet. The new buses are equipped with Series 60 Detroit Diesel 370-horsepower engines and B-500 Allison Transmissions. Van Hool, ABC Companies and Greyhound developed specifications to meet the demands of Greyhound line haul service. Interior and exterior enhancements have been made to these buses.

Greyhound Lines had emerged from bankruptcy in 1991. At that time there was a need to update its fleet of aging buses. A decision was made to update the fleet with a new bus from Motor Coach Industries (MCI), designated the Model MC-12. Except for a few cosmetic changes the MC-12 looked identical to the MCI Model MC-9. In 1992 Greyhound began adding the MC-12 to its fleet. During the next few years, 2,000 units were delivered to Greyhound. With the cost savings that resulted with the MC-12s, Greyhound was strengthened.

Greyhound Lines, Dallas, Texas, began a program of selling advertising on a limited number of its buses in 1996. The advertising involves a wrap, which covers the entire bus. The first wrapped buses were Motor Coach Industries MC-9s and MC-12s and designs featured Greyhound dogs and the Statue of Liberty. Many companies took advantage of the advertising due to the fact that Greyhound buses are very visible on America's highways.

Airport Transfer, Ltd., Halifax, Nova Scotia, operated charter and tour service under the Nova Charter Service name. Two Motor Coach Industries (MCI) Model 102C3 buses, one of which is pictured here, were delivered in 1989. Two more were added in 1990. One of the features of the 102C3 models was fully paintable sides. There was an option to have silversiding on the baggage doors. Nova Charter had this option for their buses, yet had a sizable space above for the company name.

Motor Coach Industries (MCI) launched its first 45-foot bus in 1992 on the 60th anniversary of the company. It was known as the Model 102DL3 and the new length allowed seating for 55 passengers. The Detroit Diesel Series 60 diesel engine is standard for this bus. Many intercity bus operators, including Greyhound Lines as well as charter and tour companies, added this new MCI bus to their fleets.

Motor Coach Industries (MCI) introduced the Model 102C3 in 1990. An important feature was the smooth, fully paintable sides. This enabled bus operators to feature new paint schemes on their buses. Discovery Coaches of Sheboygan, Wisconsin purchased this Model 102C3 in 1990 and applied a colorful red and orange graphic design to the exterior. Discovery Coaches began as Prigge's Charter Buses in 1949.

Many early bus companies began from horse-drawn stagecoaches or livery services. One of these companies is the Penetang Midland Coach Lines (PMCL), Midland, Ontario. It goes back to 1867 with a livery served by the Dubeau family. It was a regional bus company in the early bus days. In the 1990s it expanded, not only into charters and tours, but also in its route services. In 1993 the company acquired three Motor Coach Industries Model 102C3 buses.

Arrow Coach Lines, Little Rock, Arkansas, had its start in 1944 as a small intercity bus line operating in Arkansas and Mississippi. Later it entered into the school bus business, but eventually charter and tour service became its only business, which has proven successful. In 1994, when celebrating its 50th anniversary, Arrow Coach Lines purchased this Motor Coach Industries Model 102D3 bus.

Northwestern Stages, Spokane, Washington, took delivery of this Motor Coach Industries (MCI) Model 102D3 in 1995 to serve its intercity route between Spokane and Seattle and Tacoma. The company pioneered a route in the early 1920s and acquired a Greyhound route between Lewiston, Idaho and Spokane, Washington in the late 1980s. The MCI 102D3 was introduced in 1994 and offered a few changes over the previous C models. Primarily, the engine compartment was changed to accommodate the Series 60 Detroit Diesel four-cycle engine.

The Blue Bird Body Company, Fort Valley, Georgia, introduced the Q Bus in 1992. It was built in several sizes and used primarily for urban service. A number of bus companies bought the Q Bus for charter and tour work. Medicine Lake Bus Company, Golden Valley, Minnesota, began leasing this Q Bus in 1996 for its charter and contract work. It has a Cummins eight-liter, 250-horsepower diesel engine. The Medicine Lake Bus Company began in 1940 as a small Minneapolis area suburban bus company.

Blue Bird Body Company, Fort Valley, Georgia, a company that began in 1927, has been noted for its school buses, but it has also been building commercial buses. Another Blue Bird activity has been building motor home vehicles, and its Wanderlodge has been a big success. Using the technology and styling of the Wanderlodge, Blue Bird launched the LTC-40, a three-axle intercity bus, in 1997. In 1999 Northside Bus Service, Inc., Cape Cod, Massachusetts, purchased this Blue Bird LTC-40 bus.

Badsen Transportation, Inc., Tuscumbia, Alabama, bought this Blue Bird LTC-40 bus in 1999. It seats 45 passengers and has a Cummins M-11 450-horsepower diesel engine. Badsen has been in business since 1960 and is involved in charter and tour service. Badsen has 16 buses in its fleet, including the Blue Bird LTC-40 bus pictured here.

In 1994, Consorcio G Grupo Dina, Mexico City, Mexico, merged with Motor Coach Industries International, Des Plaines, Illinois. The manufacture of Motor Coach Industries (MCI) buses continued in Canada and the United States. Late in 1994 the MCI sales organization began marketing the Dina Viaggio model bus in the United States and Canada. The Dina Viaggio was assembled in the Dina plant in Mexico from the knocked down body shipped from the Marcopolo factory in Caxias do Sul, Brazil. A Dina Viaggio demonstrator is pictured here.

In 1998, New Flyer Industries, Winnipeg, Manitoba, introduced the Model D45S suburban bus. It was designed to attract public transit agencies, which wanted to use luxury intercity buses on longer-distance suburban commuter services. The D45S has a 45-foot length, seats up to 47 passengers, is air conditioned, and has a number of passenger comfort features. It is also equipped with a wheelchair lift. The Model D45S pictured here was demonstrated at an American Public Transit Association meeting and featured a livery for Metro in Houston, Texas.

Trans Bridge Lines, Bethlehem, Pennsylvania, was one of the first companies adding the Motor Coach Industries (MCI) Renaissance model to its fleet. The Renaissance, which became known as the Model E4500, was introduced in 1996. It had many new features including curved entrance stairs. Trans Bridge became the owner of eight E4500 buses soon after their introduction. Trans Bridge Lines has commuter service to New York City as well as a large charter and tour business. The company was founded in 1941, although its roots date back to 1915 when the founder owned a bus that transported soldiers during World War I.

Most bus manufacturers offer their buses to companies specializing in refitting the bus interiors for entertainers, businesses and individuals. John Madden, a noted sportscaster, has acquired several Motor Coach Industries (MCI) specially equipped buses with living quarters, office and other special use space. Madden's latest special MCI bus is this Renaissance Model E4500.

Motor Coach Industries (MCI) returned to the 35-foot bus market in 2000 when the Model F3500 bus was introduced. This model meets the needs of operators wanting a bus for small charter groups. It is also fulfilling requirements for airport shuttles. Ithaca (New York) Airline Limousine is one of the operators using an MCI F3500 bus for its airport shuttle service. A Cummins 285-horsepower engine powers this model.

Greyhound Canada, Calgary, Alberta, began operating Motor Coach Industries (MCI) 45-foot buses starting in 1995. A total of 97 of the Model 102DL3 were acquired between 1995 and 2001. Pictured here leaving the Lake Louise, Alberta bus station is one of the MCI 102DL3 buses Greyhound Canada added in 1998.

Greyhound Lines, Dallas, Texas, began adding 45-foot buses to its fleet in 1998. These buses were Motor Coach Industries (MCI) Model 102DL3 buses. They are mainly assigned to transcontinental services and other long-distance routes. A total of 634 of these buses were added between 1998 and 2001. Between 2001 and 2003 newer MCI 45-passenger buses, with the model designation D4500, were added for a total of 22 in all.

The G Model Motor Coach Industries bus, first introduced in 2000, was especially designed for Greyhound Lines services. Two G models are produced, a 41-foot G4100 and the 45-foot G4500. Greyhound added 11 G4100 buses in 2000 and began receiving G4500 buses in 2001. These buses have become the standard bus for Greyhound today. Pictured is a new Greyhound G4500 with new overall graphics.

The Motor Coach Industries (MCI) Model G4500 buses began to see service on Greyhound Canada routes in 2001. There were 65 G4500 buses in the first order for Greyhound Canada. A large amount of packages are carried by Calgary, Alberta-based Greyhound Canada, and because of the increased volume in recent years, trailers hooked to the rear of the buses have been utilized. Seen here is one of Greyhound Canada's new G4500 MCI buses with a trailer in tow leaving Banff, Alberta.

Prevost Car, Inc., Ste. Claire, Quebec, introduced its Model H3-40 bus in 1990. It was a completely new model bus for Prevost, although it had a styling similar to the articulated Model H5-60 presented in 1986. The H3-40 model was a high-level bus seating 48 passengers. It had European styling with a large windshield and large side windows. A Detroit Diesel 6V-92TA engine mounted in-line in the rear was the standard engine, and a Detroit Diesel 8V-92TA was available as an option.

Indian Trails, Inc., Owosso, Michigan, is one of the early pioneers in the bus industry. It began in 1910 and was originally called the Owosso-Flint Bus Line, connecting the two cities in its name. Later the company expanded to Chicago and also began serving a number of other important cities in Michigan. In 2002, Indian Trails bought six Motor Coach Industries (MCI) Model J4500 buses. Four more were added in 2003 and four more in 2004. These buses are operated in regular service, charters and tours for Tauck Tours. The J Model MCI buses feature Detroit Diesel Series 60 engines.

Prevost Car, Inc., Ste. Claire, Quebec, introduced the Le Mirage XL II model in 2000. This new bus was redesigned from the Le Mirage II. Jefferson Lines, Minneapolis, Minnesota, has five of the new Prevost Le Mirage XL II buses adding to the 11 Le Mirage II buses they acquired earlier. After a small beginning in 1919 with routes in Minnesota, Jefferson Lines has expanded over the years and now serves ten states and Manitoba, Canada.

James River Bus Lines, Richmond, Virginia, which recently celebrated 75 years in business, operates a sizable charter, tour, sightseeing and contract bus service in Virginia with a fleet of 50 buses. One of its buses is this 2003 Prevost Le Mirage XL II bus, which has joined four other Le Mirage XL II buses. Prevost Car, Inc., Ste. Claire, Quebec, introduced the model in 2000.

A new idea for a combination vehicle was presented early in 2001. It is a double-deck half bus to accommodate approximately 33 passengers, and has space on a rear platform for a freight container. Built by Neoplan, USA, Lamar, Colorado, it is one of the many innovative bus designs presented by Neoplan over the years. It is not known if any operating bus company has purchased any of these vehicles.

Bellair Charters, Ferndale, Washington, operates airport service between several Northwestern Washington cities and the Sea-Tac International Airport near Seattle. Two of these 2002 buses, with Krystal Enterprises bodies, are the types used for airport shuttles. The buses are built on International 3400 chassis. Bellair also operates charter service in the area. The company began in 1983.

In 2001, ABC Companies introduced a small, economical bus, the M1000, for charter and shuttle services. It featured body-on-chassis construction on a custom Freightliner chassis, and has been made available in 30- or 35-foot lengths and a 102-inch width. This small bus featured extra headroom and a variety of seating plans.

The Model S 417 Setra bus, built by the DaimlerChrysler Setra division in Germany, was introduced in 2002. This new bus is patterned after the Setra Top Class 400, a successful European bus. The S 417 has been designed particularly for the United States market. It has a 45-foot, 102-inch-wide body. A Detroit Diesel Series 60 engine is standard. It is sold through the Setra of North America office in Greensboro, North Carolina.

After more than six decades, the red buses of Glacier National Park continue their role in sightseeing service. From 1935 through 1937, Glacier Park, Inc., East Glacier, Montana, purchased 35 Model 709 White Motor Company buses. Then, in 2002, all but two of the original buses were donated to the National Park Foundation. Later the buses were completely refurbished by the Ford Motor Co. They looked like the 1936 buses seen in this picture, but they were new mechanically and the bodies were refurbished.

Cyr Bus Lines, Old Town, Maine, added ten Setra Model S 417 buses in 2003, soon after they became available. Cyr Bus Lines has been a good customer for Setra buses since they were first introduced to the United States by Karl Kassbohrer, AG, Stuttgart, Germany. Cyr Bus Lines follows its roots back to 1907. It is an important operator of charter tours and school buses in Maine. A route to Northern Maine is also operated.

Motor Coach Industries (MCI) has been producing Inmate Security Transport Vehicles (ISTV) for the inmate transport market since 1981. MCI is the only manufacturer of heavy-duty, three-axle, fully outfitted inmate transport vehicles in the United States and Canada. These buses are in use with federal, state, provincial and county law enforcement agencies.

New Jersey Transit (NJ Transit) is operating four new hybrid electric Motor Coach Industries (MCI) Model D4000 buses. The hybrid electric system is the newest form of propulsion for buses and it is expected to be the motive power of the future. The system for the bus includes an Allison EP50 electric drive. There are two electric motors and a small diesel engine in the system. The electric motors also serve as alternators, recharging an on-board battery pack as the buses coast or approach a stop. The NJ Transit hybrid system is the first installed in Motor Coach Industries buses.

Index

More Great Titles From Iconografix

BUSES

Buses of ACF Photo Archive Including ACF-Brill And CCF-Brill	ISBN 1-58388-101-8
Buses of Motor Coach Industries 1932-2000 Photo Archive	ISBN 1-58388-039-9
Fageol & Twin Coach Buses 1922-1956 Photo Archive	ISBN 1-58388-075-5
Flxible Intercity Buses 1924-1970 Photo Archive	ISBN 1-58388-108-5
Flxible Transit Buses 1953-1995 Photo Archive	ISBN 1-58388-053-4
GM Intercity Coaches 1944-1980 Photo Archive	ISBN 1-58388-099-2
Greyhound Buses 1914-2000 Photo Archive	ISBN 1-58388-027-5
Greyhound in Postcards: Buses, Depots and Posthouses	ISBN 1-58388-130-1
Highway Buses of the 20th Century Photo Gallery	ISBN 1-58388-121-2
Mack® Buses 1900-1960 Photo Archive*	ISBN 1-58388-020-8
Prevost Buses 1924-2002 Photo Archive	ISBN 1-58388-083-6
Trailways Buses 1936-2001 Photo Archive	ISBN 1-58388-029-1
Trolley Buses 1913-2001 Photo Archive	ISBN 1-58388-057-7
Yellow Coach Buses 1923-1943 Photo Archive	ISBN 1-58388-054-2

RECREATIONAL VEHICLES

RVs & Campers 1900-2000: An Illustrated History	ISBN 1-58388-064-X
Ski-Doo Racing Sleds 1960-2003 Photo Archive	ISBN 1-58388-105-0

TRUCKS

Autocar Trucks 1899-1950 Photo Archive	ISBN 1-58388-115-8
Autocar Trucks 1950-1987 Photo Archive	ISBN 1-58388-072-0
Beverage Trucks 1910-1975 Photo Archive	ISBN 1-882256-60-3
Brockway Trucks 1948-1961 Photo Archive*	ISBN 1-882256-55-7
Chevrolet El Camino Photo History Incl. GMC Sprint & Caballero	ISBN 1-58388-044-5
Circus and Carnival Trucks 1923-2000 Photo Archive	ISBN 1-58388-048-8
Dodge B-Series Trucks Restorer's & Collector's Reference Guide and History	ISBN 1-58388-087-9
Dodge Pickups 1939-1978 Photo Album	ISBN 1-882256-82-4
Dodge Power Wagons 1940-1980 Photo Archive	ISBN 1-882256-89-1
Dodge Power Wagon Photo History	ISBN 1-58388-019-4
Dodge Ram Trucks 1994-2001 Photo History	ISBN 1-58388-051-8
Dodge Trucks 1929-1947 Photo Archive	ISBN 1-882256-36-0
Dodge Trucks 1948-1960 Photo Archive	ISBN 1-882256-37-9
Ford 4x4s 1935-1990 Photo History	ISBN 1-58388-079-8
Ford Heavy-Duty Trucks 1948-1998 Photo History	ISBN 1-58388-043-7
Ford Ranchero 1957-1979 Photo History	ISBN 1-58388-126-3
Freightliner Trucks 1937-1981 Photo Archive	ISBN 1-58388-090-9
GMC Heavy-Duty Trucks 1927-1987	ISBN 1-58388-125-5
Jeep 1941-2000 Photo Archive	ISBN 1-58388-021-6
Jeep Prototypes & Concept Vehicles Photo Archive	ISBN 1-58388-033-X
Mack Model AB Photo Archive*	ISBN 1-882256-18-2
Mack AP Super-Duty Trucks 1926-1938 Photo Archive*	ISBN 1-882256-54-9
Mack Model B 1953-1966 Volume 2 Photo Archive*	ISBN 1-882256-34-4
Mack EB-EC-ED-EE-EF-EG-DE 1936-1951 Photo Archive*	ISBN 1-882256-29-8
Mack EH-EJ-EM-EQ-ER-ES 1936-1950 Photo Archive*	ISBN 1-882256-39-5
Mack FC-FCSW-NW 1936-1947 Photo Archive*	ISBN 1-882256-28-X
Mack FG-FH-FJ-FK-FN-FP-FT-FW 1937-1950 Photo Archive*	ISBN 1-882256-35-2
Mack LF-LH-LJ-LM-LT 1940-1956 Photo Archive*	ISBN 1-882256-38-7
Mack Trucks Photo Gallery*	ISBN 1-882256-88-3
New Car Carriers 1910-1998 Photo Album	ISBN 1-882256-98-0
Plymouth Commercial Vehicles Photo Archive	ISBN 1-58388-004-6
Refuse Trucks Photo Archive	ISBN 1-58388-042-9
Studebaker Trucks 1927-1940 Photo Archive	ISBN 1-882256-40-9
White Trucks 1900-1937 Photo Archive	ISBN 1-882256-80-8

EMERGENCY VEHICLES

The American Ambulance 1900-2002: An Illustrated History	ISBN 1-58388-081-X
American Fire Apparatus Co. 1922-1993 Photo Archive	ISBN 1-58388-131-X
American Funeral Vehicles 1883-2003 Illustrated History	ISBN 1-58388-104-2
American LaFrance 700 Series 1945-1952 Photo Archive	ISBN 1-882256-90-5
American LaFrance 700 Series 1945-1952 Photo Archive Volume 2	ISBN 1-58388-025-9
American LaFrance 700 & 800 Series 1953-1958 Photo Archive	ISBN 1-882256-91-3
American LaFrance 900 Series 1958-1964 Photo Archive	ISBN 1-58388-002-X
Classic Seagrave 1935-1951 Photo Archive	ISBN 1-58388-034-8
Crown Firecoach 1951-1985 Photo Archive	ISBN 1-58388-047-X
Encyclopedia of Canadian Fire Apparatus	ISBN 1-58388-119-0
Fire Chief Cars 1900-1997 Photo Album	ISBN 1-882256-87-5
Hahn Fire Apparatus 1923-1990 Photo Archive	ISBN 1-58388-077-1
Heavy Rescue Trucks 1931-2000 Photo Gallery	ISBN 1-58388-045-3
Imperial Fire Apparatus 1969-1976 Photo Archive	ISBN 1-58388-091-7
Industrial and Private Fire Apparatus 1925-2001 Photo Archive	ISBN 1-58388-049-6
Mack Model C Fire Trucks 1957-1967 Photo Archive*	ISBN 1-58388-014-3
Mack Model L Fire Trucks 1940-1954 Photo Archive*	ISBN 1-882256-86-7
Maxim Fire Apparatus 1914-1989 Photo Archive	ISBN 1-58388-050-X
Maxim Fire Apparatus Photo History	ISBN 1-58388-111-5
Navy & Marine Corps Fire Apparatus 1836 -2000 Photo Gallery	ISBN 1-58388-031-3
Pierre Thibault Ltd. Fire Apparatus 1918-1990 Photo Archive	ISBN 1-58388-074-7
Pirsch Fire Apparatus 1890-1991 Photo Archive	ISBN 1-58388-082-8
Police Cars: Restoring, Collecting & Showing America's Finest Sedans	ISBN 1-58388-046-1
Saulsbury Fire Rescue Apparatus 1956-2003 Photo Archive	ISBN 1-58388-106-9
Seagrave 70th Anniversary Series Photo Archive	ISBN 1-58388-001-1
Seagrave Fire Apparatus 1959-2004 Photo Archive	ISBN 1-58388-132-8
TASC Fire Apparatus 1946-1985 Photo Archive	ISBN 1-58388-065-8
Volunteer & Rural Fire Apparatus Photo Gallery	ISBN 1-58388-005-4
W.S. Darley & Co. Fire Apparatus 1908-2000 Photo Archive	ISBN 1-58388-061-5
Wildland Fire Apparatus 1940-2001 Photo Gallery	ISBN 1-58388-056-9
Young Fire Equipment 1932-1991 Photo Archive	ISBN 1-58388-015-1

RAILWAYS

Burlington Zephyrs Photo Archive: America's Distinctive Trains	ISBN 1-58388-124-7
Chicago, St. Paul, Minneapolis & Omaha Railway 1880-1940 Photo Archive	ISBN 1-58388-067-0
Chicago & North Western Railway 1975-1995 Photo Archive	ISBN 1-882256-76-X
Classic Sreamliners Photo Archive: The Trains and the Designers	ISBN 1-58388-144-x
Great Northern Railway 1945-1970 Volume 2 Photo Archive	ISBN 1-882256-79-4
Great Northern Railway Ore Docks of Lake Superior Photo Archive	ISBN 1-58388-073-9
Illinois Central Railroad 1854-1960 Photo Archive	ISBN 1-58388-063-3
Locomotives of the Upper Midwest Photo Archive: Diesel Power in the 1960s and 1970s	ISBN 1-58388-113-1
Milwaukee Road 1850-1960 Photo Archive	ISBN 1-882256-61-1
Milwaukee Road Depots 1856-1954 Photo Archive	ISBN 1-58388-040-2
Show Trains of the 20th Century	ISBN 1-58388-030-5
Soo Line 1975-1992 Photo Archive	ISBN 1-882256-68-9
Steam Locomotives of the B&O Railroad Photo Archive	ISBN 1-58388-095-X
Streamliners to the Twin Cities Photo Archive 400, Twin Zephyrs & Hiawatha Trains	ISBN 1-58388-096-8
Trains of the Twin Ports Photo Archive, Duluth-Superior in the 1950s	ISBN 1-58388-003-8
Trains of the Circus 1872-1956	ISBN 1-58388-024-0
Trains of the Upper Midwest Photo Archive Steam & Diesel in the 1950s & 1960s	ISBN 1-58388-036-4
Wisconsin Central Limited 1987-1996 Photo Archive	ISBN 1-882256-75-1
Wisconsin Central Railway 1871-1909 Photo Archive	ISBN 1-882256-78-6

AMERICAN CULTURE

Coca-Cola: Its Vehicles in Photographs 1930-1969	ISBN 1-882256-47-6
Phillips 66 1945-1954 Photo Archive	ISBN 1-882256-42-5

AUTOMOTIVE

AMC Cars 1954-1987: An Illustrated History	ISBN 1-58388-112-3
AMC Performance Cars 1951-1983 Photo Archive	ISBN 1-58388-127-1
AMX Photo Archive: From Concept to Reality	ISBN 1-58388-062-3
Auburn Automobiles 1900-1936 Photo Archive	ISBN 1-58388-093-3
Camaro 1967-2000 Photo Archive	ISBN 1-58388-032-1
Checker Cab Co. Photo History	ISBN 1-58388-100-X
Chevrolet Corvair Photo History	ISBN 1-58388-118-2
Chevrolet Station Wagons 1946-1966 Photo Archive	ISBN 1-58388-069-0
Classic American Limousines 1955-2000 Photo Archive	ISBN 1-58388-041-0
Cord Automobiles L-29 & 810/812 Photo Archive	ISBN 1-58388-102-6
Corvair by Chevrolet Experimental & Production Cars 1957-1969, Ludvigsen Library Series	ISBN 1-58388-058-5
Corvette The Exotic Experimental Cars, Ludvigsen Library Series	ISBN 1-58388-017-8
Corvette Prototypes & Show Cars Photo Album	ISBN 1-882256-77-8
Early Ford V-8s 1932-1942 Photo Album	ISBN 1-882256-97-2
Ferrari- The Factory Maranello's Secrets 1950-1975, Ludvigsen Library Series	ISBN 1-58388-085-2
Ford Postwar Flatheads 1946-1953 Photo Archive	ISBN 1-58388-080-1
Ford Station Wagons 1929-1991 Photo History	ISBN 1-58388-103-4
Hudson Automobiles 1934-1957 Photo Archive	ISBN 1-58388-110-7
Imperial 1955-1963 Photo Archive	ISBN 1-882256-22-0
Imperial 1964-1968 Photo Archive	ISBN 1-882256-23-9
Javelin Photo Archive: From Concept to Reality	ISBN 1-58388-071-2
Lincoln Motor Cars 1920-1942 Photo Archive	ISBN 1-882256-57-3
Lincoln Motor Cars 1946-1960 Photo Archive	ISBN 1-882256-58-1
Nash 1936-1957 Photo Archive	ISBN 1-58388-086-0
Packard Motor Cars 1935-1942 Photo Archive	ISBN 1-882256-44-1
Packard Motor Cars 1946-1958 Photo Archive	ISBN 1-882256-45-X
Pontiac Dream Cars, Show Cars & Prototypes 1928-1998 Photo Album	ISBN 1-882256-93-X
Pontiac Firebird Trans-Am 1969-1999 Photo Album	ISBN 1-882256-95-6
Pontiac Firebird 1967-2000 Photo History	ISBN 1-58388-028-3
Rambler 1950-1969 Photo Archive	ISBN 1-58388-078-X
Stretch Limousines 1928-2001 Photo Archive	ISBN 1-58388-070-4
Studebaker 1933-1942 Photo Archive	ISBN 1-882256-24-7
Studebaker Hawk 1956-1964 Photo Archive	ISBN 1-58388-094-1
Studebaker Lark 1959-1966 Photo Archive	ISBN 1-58388-107-7
Ultimate Corvette Trivia Challenge	ISBN 1-58388-035-6

More great books from **Iconografix**

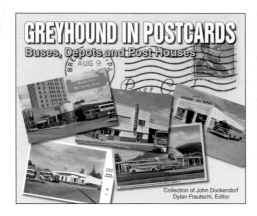
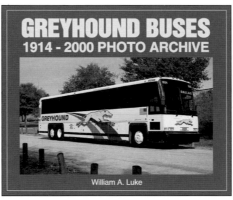
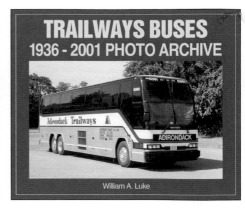
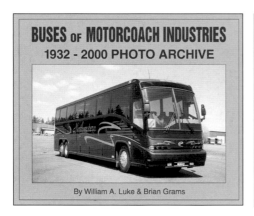
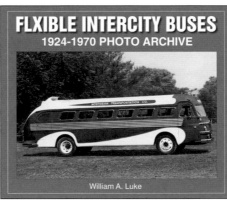
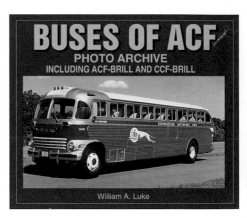
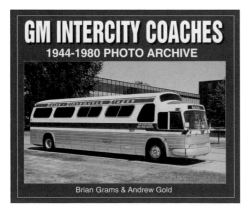